ENDORSEMENTS

As laborers in glass houses, Public Servants are often intimidated into hiding their faith under a bushel. Sadly, this is dishonoring to our Lord, who has enlarged our borders for opportunities to influence. Sad, because it diminishes our ability to communicate the reason for the faith, hope, and love that is hopefully flowing from us to those who watch us. Ralph Drollinger's *Oaks in Office: Biblical Essays for Political Leaders* provides a road map whereby men and women come to understand the role and responsibility we have as believers in the public arena. His deep-dive studies, born of years of Biblical studies and interface with Public Servants at all levels, teach us how to become more effective missionaries, irrespective of partisanship or political views, in our own sphere of influence. I can unequivocally recommend *Oaks in Office* to those who want to know more about how a Christ follower can be true to their Lord while being effective in their public duties.

— **SONNY PERDUE** FORMER GOVERNOR OF GEORGIA

Oaks in Office is a wonderful gift from Ralph Drollinger, who has dedicated much of his life to Public Servants who wish to maintain and enhance their faith and character while navigating the often complex landscape of government life. It is a scholarly yet easily understood tome with great lessons for everyone.

— **DR. BENJAMIN S. CARSON SR., MD**

I was a successful Eagle Scout because a Scoutmaster guided me through the Boy Scouts of America manual. I was a proficient Air Force pilot because an instructor taught me how to use a checklist. Ralph Drollinger is my life instructor, leading me and many other Public Servants through the most important checklist in history. Capitol Ministries'® work delving into Biblical truths is creating mighty Oaks in Office around the world. I suppose Ralph's figurative cultivation, fertilization, and watering is making him the equivalent of a Biblical Johnny Appleseed!

— **RICK PERRY** FORMER GOVERNOR OF TEXAS

The political noise in our nation's capital can often distract us from what's really important. Ralph Drollinger's *Oaks in Office*, and the Bible study Ralph and Danielle lead every week, help keep us focused on God and His direction.

— **U.S. SENATOR DAVID PERDUE**, GA

Oaks in Office works through the difficult issues and the awesome responsibility of representing Him while holding public office. From the basic question, should believers be involved in politics? to informing public policy with Biblical principles, to practical issues involved with living a public life, *Oaks in Office* gives thought-provoking insights.

— **U.S. SENATOR WILLIAM CASSIDY**, LA

The best hour of my week is the Senate Bible Study. In a world starved for truth, we desperately need more *Oaks in Office*. I'm grateful for Ralph and Danielle's faithfulness to do just that.

— **U.S. SENATOR STEVE DAINES**, MT

Praying for those in authority is a Biblical mandate, just like the mandate to make disciples. There is no question that it is easier to pray for a leader than it is to help him become a disciple. This book is about the tough and joyous work of making disciples of all nations and the leaders of those nations. When leaders have a solid Biblical core, their family, community, and decisions are forever changed.

— **U.S. SENATOR JAMES LANKFORD**, OK

Elected Public Servants have been given a great responsibility and charge—to care for their fellow man. Whether a first-time member of the county livestock board or the United States House of Representatives, the tasks and challenges that arise can seem daunting. As Ralph Drollinger proclaims throughout *Oaks in Office*, grounding in the truth of God's Word and teachings builds a deep-rooted foundation that will stand up to the most challenging of days and events in office. Through the studies contained within *Oaks in Office*, Drollinger teaches that a deep understanding and relationship with God is an asset unlike any other. It provides counsel in times of need, joy and motivation in times of great distress. In an ever-increasingly convoluted world, Drollinger's framework grounds and guides development not only as a Christian, but also as a Public Servant.
— **STEVE PEARCE** U.S. REPRESENTATIVE, NM, 2ND CONGRESSIONAL DISTRICT

I am deeply appreciative of Ralph Drollinger for the insights he offers in *Oaks in Office*. He eloquently writes that ministering to those in public service is not only about evangelizing, but also about the continued individual spiritual growth for those called to serve. Spiritual growth is always a journey. The special circumstances and challenges that face Public Servants require nurturing, similar to that which allows a fragile acorn to one day become a mighty oak. Such reflections of personal growth through study and prayer are found in Drollinger's *Oaks in Office*.
— **GLENN "GT" THOMPSON** U.S. REPRESENTATIVE, PA, 5TH CONGRESSIONAL DISTRICT

Ralph Drollinger's *Oaks In Office* is a must read for any Public Servants, especially those who believe that faith and freedom are inextricably linked. I have sat under Ralph's spiritual mentorship for most of the last eight years, and his unique ability to show how God's Word speaks to the many intricate policy issues facing America today has served to inform my work as a Member of Congress. From what the Bible says about basic human rights, to the characteristics of true leaders, to national security, to mundane policy issues like budgets, taxes, and formulating laws, his insights remind me that faith and freedom do, indeed, go hand in hand. I commend *Oaks In Office* to any Public Servant who truly desires to positively influence the cities, states, nations, and world around us in a Godly manner.
— **BILL JOHNSON** U.S. REPRESENTATIVE, OH, 6TH CONGRESSIONAL DISTRICT

Ralph Drollinger is the best Bible teacher I've studied with, and I've been blessed with many great teachers over three and a half decades as a Christian. Studying the Bible with Ralph and his wife, Danielle, is the highlight for me every week when I'm at the United States Capitol. Paul told the Corinthians that he gave them "milk" and not "solid food" when he ministered to them. Ralph never serves milk in his studies but delivers a huge serving of steak! I say this literally as he does serve us steak each week, but more importantly, his Bible studies are the most spiritually and intellectually challenging I've participated in. For starters, while I can listen and understand some five-syllable words, he speaks them fluently and with the utmost precision. I know the book *Oaks in Office* will help many elected and appointed political leaders grow in their faith in Christ and will make better disciples in our national and state capitals. We need more lights shining bright and more ambassadors for Christ in government, and *Oaks in Office* will help many of our leaders get off the milk diets and eating solid foods!
— **DON BACON** U.S. REPRESENTATIVE, NE, 2ND CONGRESSIONAL DISTRICT

Public Servants are uniquely positioned to influence culture, both through legislation and as they live their lives under the microscope of public scrutiny. Ralph Drollinger understands the pressures and challenges facing public officials. Over the years, Ralph has offered consistent encouragement and spiritual insight through his Bible studies, counsel, and prayer. Ralph has gained great esteem and respect from elected officials all over the U.S. and indeed all over the world. I pray that *Oaks in Office* will be used to bring a spiritual reawakening to those in public office, and that Public Servants might be a part of rejuvenating the heart and soul of the United States of America.
— **DOUG LAMBORN** U.S. REPRESENTATIVE, CO, 5TH CONGRESSIONAL DISTRICT

I appreciate Ralph Drollinger and Capitol Ministries®. The Bible studies go in depth on issues we as legislators face daily; always referring back to the foundational principles contained in the Scriptures. And for this I am grateful.
— **MIKE MORRELL** MEMBER OF THE CALIFORNIA STATE SENATE, 23RD DISTRICT

Our nation was built upon the Word of God. Our founders and the people they governed understood they must be led by godly people, who while imperfect themselves, strived to build a country based on God's perfection. Today, in a country where God's Word is under constant attack, we need mighty Oaks to serve in all levels of government. Men and women of courage and commitment who will stand for the principles and values our nation was founded upon. Ralph Drollinger's book, *Oaks in Office*, clearly lays out who is needed and what is needed to guide our nation to greatness so we can be the light of the world that God intended us to be. Matthew 20:26

— **DAN PATRICK** LIEUTENANT GOVERNOR, TX

From the perspective of a city councilman who is somewhat controversial because I stand up for "Life, Liberty, and the Pursuit of Happiness (property rights)," this book should be mandatory reading. Knowing that God is the originator of property rights, and not government and not a majority of voters, allows me to stand firm against what I refer to as the noisy minority. Imagine if people couldn't keep the fruits of their labor, or if your neighbors could decide whether you could remodel your kitchen! Knowing God's design for government is what *Oaks in Office* is all about. Every Office Holder ought to have this book.

—**SCOTT PEOTTER** CITY COUNCILMAN, NEWPORT BEACH, CA

The Great Commission is all about making disciples in all nations. God has used Ralph Drollinger and Capitol Ministries® to provide a strategic initiative to infiltrate all the world capitals with an exciting disciple-making ministry. *Oaks in Office* provides national ministries in these capitals with significant resources to make disciples among the Public Servants in capitols around the world.

— **PAUL CEDAR** PAST EXECUTIVE CHAIR, LAUSANNE MOVEMENT

Oaks in Office provides a Biblically grounded expression for Public Servants to be salt and light in the public square. It is a guidebook for all who have a passion to expand Christ's kingdom and to further the public good. Ralph Drollinger has tested and integrated these Biblical truths so they can be applied in the halls of Congress, the steps of the Capitol, and even the gathering places in your home. I pray for the courage of public leaders to read, examine, and engage in living out the challenges of this book, for the good of all and the glory of God.

— **TOM DE VRIES** PRESIDENT/CEO, WILLOW CREEK ASSOCIATION

Evangelical pastors as a whole have largely overlooked the importance of building effective ministries that disciple local government leaders for Christ. With over 40,000 local governments in America we need to birth ministries similar to what Youth for Christ and CRU are doing on high school and college campuses. If we are to truly "Make America Great Again," initiating these kinds of outposts is essential. Statistics indicate that most of our political leaders in state capitals and Washington D.C. were once city council members. In *Oaks in Office* Ralph Drollinger provides an invaluable tool to equip pastors and laymen with pertinent Bible studies to initiate discipleship ministries with those serving in local government. I highly recommend this excellent resource.

— **DR. ROBERT JEFFRESS** SENIOR PASTOR, FIRST BAPTIST CHURCH, DALLAS, TX; BIBLE TEACHER ON *PATHWAY TO VICTORY*

Isaiah 61:3 says, "... ***So they will be called oaks of righteousness, the planting of the LORD, that He may be glorified.***" Our country may have many issues today that need immediate attention, but we do have one huge advantage: followers of Christ occupying governmental positions that provide opportunities to make a positive difference in our society. If you serve as one of these public officials, regardless of office, you should read and apply the sound Biblical teachings found in *Oaks in Office*. As you do so, you will grow into a strong oak of righteousness that brings much glory to God because you will begin to serve as His representative, exerting a godly influence on our country.

— **DR. BILL JONES** CHANCELLOR, COLUMBIA INTERNATIONAL UNIVERSITY

Always there have been *Oaks in Office*, men and women whose lives have shouted integrity through the halls of Congress or the state house. But there has not been a time since the Civil War when America so needed mighty Oaks who cared not for their careers but only sought the heart of God and the good of the people. Ralph Drollinger's monograph of that arresting title has grasped the need of the hour in a volume that you cannot put down. As a favor to your country and as a boon to your prayer life, read this volume and thank God that someone understands and has the courage to put this in print.

— **DR. PAIGE PATTERSON** PRESIDENT, SOUTHWESTERN BAPTIST THEOLOGICAL SEMINARY, FORT WORTH, TX

Ralph Drollinger's book, *Oaks in Office*, is based on his many years of impactful ministry with key state and national political leaders. The chapters are carefully Biblical, theologically correct, and strategically practical. Highly recommended.
— **DR. LARRY PETTEGREW** PROVOST AND DEAN, SHEPHERDS THEOLOGICAL SEMINARY

Ralph Drollinger's *Oaks in Office* is a wonderful collection of 52 leadership Bible studies on pertinent issues of the day from "The Remedy for Racism" to "Sexual Sin and the Aphrodisiac of Power." This book is not just for those in elected office; I recommend it for anyone in leadership who wants to leave a legacy for the next generation. From tiny acorns, great oak trees grow and the weekly lessons in this book will be the light, water, and soil you need. If you want to be an oak in your position, get this book and apply it regularly.
— **GORDON ROBERTSON** CEO, THE CHRISTIAN BROADCASTING NETWORK

Serving as a Public Servant requires dedication, excellent skills, and godly wisdom. In his book, *Oaks in Office*, Ralph provides invaluable Biblical studies that will encourage Public Servants to increase their understanding of godly wisdom. Ralph skillfully applies Biblical themes and principles to the challenges that Public Servants face on a regular basis. His insightful and trustworthy explanation of the Biblical teaching is another strength of this book. I recommend pastors who have Public Servants in their congregation also read Ralph's book so they can gain a better understanding of how to minister to these servants of God.
— **DR. CRAIG WILLIFORD** PRESIDENT, MULTNOMAH UNIVERSITY

OAKS
IN OFFICE

OAKS
IN OFFICE

BIBLICAL ESSAYS FOR POLITICAL LEADERS

RALPH DROLLINGER

FOREWORD BY MIKE HUCKABEE

VOLUME **01**

Nordskog Publishing Inc.

Ventura, California

OAKS IN OFFICE: BIBLICAL ESSAYS FOR POLITICAL LEADERS

by Ralph Drollinger

Copyright © 2018 by Ralph Drollinger

ISBN: 978-1-946497-15-4
Library of Congress Control Number: 2018939081

Project Editor, Michelle Shelfer, benediction.biz | Proofreader, Cheryl Geyer | Designer, Leslie Colgin

Printed in the United States of America by Jostens, Inc.

Published by

Nordskog Publishing, Inc.
2716 Sailor Avenue, Ventura, California 93001
1-805-642-2070 • 1-805-276-5129
NordskogPublishing.com

MEMBER

CHRISTIAN SMALL
PUBLISHERS ASSOCIATION

DEDICATION

To Danielle, my faithful wife, who is not only my soul mate in life, but partner in ministry. You are the best thing that has ever happened to me this side of heaven—and without you, Capitol Ministries® and *Oaks in Office* would be non-existent.

CONTENTS

VOLUME **01**

VOLUME 02

VOLUME 03

VOLUME 04

FOREWORD

Staying true to one's faith and following Jesus Christ is difficult enough, but to do it while serving in the shark-infested waters of public office requires the help and encouragement of mentors whose only agenda is to provide spiritual counsel in total confidence. Ralph Drollinger is not a household name and that's the way he likes it. Although he walks and talks with the most powerful men and women in the nation and leads three separate weekly Bible Studies for Members of the White House Cabinet, Senate, and House in Washington, he does it behind the curtain so as to protect the confidence of those he ministers to.

Drollinger's new book, *Oaks in Office*, gives the reader a glimpse into what can make a powerful person yield to Christ and seek to live with integrity and honor. But you don't have to be a White House Cabinet Member, Senator, Congressman, or a Governor to be blessed by *Oaks in Office*. Jump headfirst into this great series and get a blessing intended for rulers, but applicable to all.

— **MIKE HUCKABEE** AR GOV 1996–2007, AUTHOR, HOST OF *HUCKABEE* ON TBN

Oaks are amazing trees. We have several huge oaks bordering our primary residence in Southern California. Oaks, I believe, provide a great metaphor for mature-in-Christ Public Servants. Their roots go deep, they possess internal fortitude, and their leaves do not wither (cf. Psalm 1). They stand up to drought, fire, wind, and floods. They are statuesque and noble, providing strength and shelter to their surrounding environs. They are a fitting picture of what God desires of His servants whom He has placed in public office.

The mighty oak tree spends the majority of its strength fortifying its infrastructure so that its roots will sustain the long sweeping branches that it will push up to twenty-five feet outward and parallel to the ground. It drives its roots deep into the earth, anchoring it firmly so it may stand steadfast in powerful storms that topple other weaker trees around it. Only a small bit of its energy is spent on external growth, expanding its trunk and stretching its boughs toward the sky.

It is our prayer to mature the Christian Public Servant in this way, with the development of the inner person. A steady diet of sound Biblical doctrine will grow Public Servants in their faith. Regular Bible study will help them develop critical discernment that will guide and sustain them in battles over controversial and trendy issues. Anchored in truth and righteousness, they will stand resolute and unwavering amid the storms of political debate. Scriptural Truth and God's precepts that have rooted in their hearts will lead them as they create public policy. This is our prayer and the reason for this book.

Since 1996 I have been writing in-depth Bible studies for Public Servants. Back then, my wife Danielle was the executive director of a powerful political action committee (PAC) in California that had as its primary objective to recruit, train, and help believers get elected to the legislative body of the state of California. This all occurred during what was commonly known as "the Gingrich revolution" in Washington D.C. Her PAC rode that wave of change, investing in and winning thirty-six political races in the California legislative body over a six-year period, or three election cycles.

But it was obvious something was lacking from their formula and their attempt to change the direction of California. The Members they had helped get elected, many being very young in Christ, seemed to go to Sacramento and then not make any difference. In fact, some who were elected seemed to lose their testimony for Christ altogether while being away from their home, church, and environs, for four days a week, seven to eight months a year. Danielle was frustrated with this outcome.

At the same time, I was heavily involved in the American sports ministry movement that was booming. I was serving as the president of the trade organization of America's sports ministries. In our organization, thousands of churches were represented that were using sports to grow their congregations, and eighty-four national parachurch sports ministries had been created through their auspices—outposts for Christ on most every high school, college, and professional sports team in America—placing fulltime chaplains, or better, Bible teacher/disciple-makers on those teams, pinpointing their ministry to evangelize and build athletes in Christ. The American sports ministry movement was wildly successful in reaching athletes for Christ and still flourishes to this day through ongoing well-established parachurch ministries such as the Fellowship of Christian Athletes, Athletes in Action, and Pro Athletes Outreach.

One day it dawned on Danielle and me that, given her realization that political leaders needed someone to minister to them while in office—a Bible teacher, if you will, on their Capitol campus—and my proficiencies in understanding how that is best accomplished, at least in the athletic world, we could form a new ministry organization that would create outposts for Christ on the campuses of political leaders! To our knowledge going in, nothing of that sort that was true to Scripture existed; we would later find out that was indeed true. In America there were only three state capitals with disciple-making ministries.

In 1996, sensing a very strong call of God, both of us quit our jobs to found Capitol Ministries® in the California State Capitol.

In those twelve ensuing years of ministry in the California Capitol, I found that written Bible studies were necessary in order to best serve Members of the California Assembly, Senate, and Constitutional Officers who might not otherwise, due to schedules, be able to attend our weekly Members Bible studies in the capital.

As I began the discipline of writing in-depth Bible studies every week—studies that were not only exegetically sound, but contained an application relevant to a Public Servant—I soon realized that there were little if any equivalent materials available.

All the more, I began to form earnest convictions that if our state and national leaders did not have a clear understanding of what God's Word has to say regarding matters, they could not possibly be expected to lead in the best possible direction. This is especially true as our culture slips away from its Judeo-Christian heritage and culture and into postmodern secularism. And in fact, fewer and fewer churches serve a high-protein diet of the Word of God to their congregants, resulting in even the best Christian Public Servants being woefully untaught in the precepts of God's Word. Sobering to this reality in my California capital ministry created a deep unction in my heart as to how important my Bible teaching ministry was—or at least should be to the lawmaking process—and how important written Bible studies are to the life of overbooked Public Servants. To use the summary thoughts of Chuck Colson in this regard, he stated it best I think when he said that in essence the Bible and Bible studies are "pre-political." What Colson meant by that coined word is this: that before the political process begins, every legislator and every Public Servant should know what the Bible has to say regarding a given matter. How can one possibly expect to have a state or nation that is based in Biblical precepts if the leader doesn't know what the Word of God says about a matter?

It is now twenty-one years later as I publish *Oaks In Office* with Nordskog Publishing, Inc. Having written hundreds of Bible studies aimed at helping Public Servants know the mind of God on matters, I have chosen fifty-two of those studies that I believe are most pertinent to their understanding and growth.

As you will notice from studying the Table of Contents, I have created sections that build on one another. The progression of the material suggests that the spiritual maturity and character formation of the Public Servant leads to the development of godly positions on issues while serving in office. Becoming sustaining, strongly influential Oaks in Office has much more to do with simply being Biblical on the issues. That is why before and after Part IV, "Building Biblically Based Convictions About Today's Issues," there is much content intended to forge Biblical character in the life of the political leader. This cannot be overstated. It is critically important to the direction of the nation that every elected or appointed official does not do what is "*right in his own eyes*" (Judges 21:25), but rather that they bring every vote "*captive to the obedience of Christ*" (2 Corinthians 10:5). But perhaps of even greater importance is the formation of Christlikeness in the life of the individual. There is found the sustainability necessary for godly influence in office. *Oaks in Office* therefore addresses both personal godliness and corporate righteousness.

By God's doing, it is now twenty-one years from the time Danielle and I birthed Capitol Ministries® in the California State Capitol. Since then we have watched our Lord birth many more ministries in other U.S. State capitals and Federal capitals throughout the world with similar emphasis on teaching the Word of God and making disciples. In fact, we are now in Washington D.C., where I have had the God-given privilege of teaching weekly Bible studies to a majority of the Members of the White House Cabinet, many Senators, and many House Members. This advancement of the ministry is not my doing, but God's. And it has been quite the ride, quite the adventure! Capitol Ministries® and its expansion have much more to do with God honoring the explication of His Word than it does with me and my limited abilities. To Him be the glory!

It is appropriate and customary in a tome like this to thank God for the tremendous influences He has placed in my life that have in a human sense equipped me for such a task as this. Those influences that follow are in no particular order of importance. Coach John Wooden of UCLA fame, for whom I had the privilege of playing as a member of his last two national championship teams. Coach was hugely influential in my character formation, understanding of industriousness and the necessity of preparedness. Dr. Bill Bright, whom I had the privilege of serving and being on his staff for many years through playing basketball for Athletes in Action (a ministry of then Campus Crusade for Christ, now CRU), during my sports ministry days. Dr. Bright hugely influenced the visionary side of my thinking and ministry, creating in me by his modeling a capacity, understanding, and confidence that God can use ordinary people to reach around the globe with the Gospel. He taught me not to think small, but to trust God for things beyond personal ability and comprehension. Dr. John MacArthur, who personally gave me a passion and ability through his seminary, The Master's Seminary, to carefully, skillfully, and responsibly exegete the Word of God with week-in and week-out tenacity and precision. He created a realization in me best summarized many, many years ago by the personal words of my friend, Dr. David Jeremiah: "Ralph, God honors His Word. Therefore be about explicating His Word if you expect Him to increase your ministry."

I would like to think that I am a combination, to a much lesser degree, of these individuals and their respective strengths. Apart from Christ, they are the human influences He has given me whom I continually model after the most. They have been the underlying influences that help to explain best what Capitol Ministries® is all about, and I thank God for allowing me to rub shoulders over many, many years with each of them.

My prayer is that *Oaks in Office* will be used by God to help shape the character and direction of the next generation of political leaders, not only in America but throughout the world. Presently my weekly written Bible studies are translated into several other languages, and it is our hope and prayer that *Oaks in Office* will soon be translated into other languages as well for use in our emerging and growing international ministries.

Here then are fifty-two of my most pertinent Bible studies, reformatted into book form, that are intended to be the training curriculum not only for existing political leaders but even more for the next generation of leaders—the up-and-coming Public Servants. May God use *Oaks in Office* to form a Christian worldview in those who have emerging political careers, those men and women who will someday lead our great nation and other nations as well.

Oaks in Office is particularly designed to be used by Capitol Ministries'® trained ministry leaders who sense a call to reach local government leaders for Christ. We call this division of our ministry CivicReach® and we have produced *Oaks in Office* primarily for them: to equip CivicReach® leaders with good Bible-study materials that are custom-designed to best minister to up-and-coming political leaders who desire to please God with their life and service. Enjoy the book if you are one of these people reading this! Our most focused prayer is that God will use *Oaks in Office* to mature you in Christ as you serve Him in His institution of Civil Government.

RALPH DROLLINGER
capmin.org

ACKNOWLEDGEMENTS

A special thank you to those who have helped bring this tome to life. First and foremost, to Deborah Mendenhall, who has for years tirelessly edited and critiqued the weekly Bibles studies that I write—fifty-two eight- to twelve-page studies per year—for our teaching ministry in Washington D.C. to Members of the White House Cabinet, U.S. Senate, and House. The fifty-two chapters herein are derived from those studies that Deb has scrubbed into shape with me through a back-and-forth electronic volley, as I travel almost all of the time. Deb's editing skills are of tremendous value to me and to our ministry. In the same vein, I must give special thanks to Michelle Shelfer, the lead editor at Nordskog Publishing, whose skills at adapting my Bible-study manuscripts and combing them into book form have proven invaluable. I am so grateful too for Leslie Colgin, our graphic designer. I have known Leslie since she was a little baby (one of the daughters of Linus Morris, who discipled me when I was a student at UCLA). I have watched Leslie grow up, not only physically and spiritually, but vocationally. A highly skilled and talented designer, she has taken *Oaks in Office* under her care and created a layout that is not only attractive, but workable for all who are desirous of interacting with the content. I've greatly relied on the mature Christian insight and knowledge of Dan Madison, who has tirelessly pored over the manuscripts for theological correctness and clarity. His contributions have been abundant and valuable. A very special thanks as well is in order to Jerry Nordskog, who has published many other books in this genre and who has given me the opportunity to create written materials that are not only exegetically drilled down, but specifically applicable to the lives of Public Servants and leaders worldwide. Not every publisher is interested in such a narrow bandwidth for a publication. Nonetheless, Jerry saw the void in this area and caught the strategic importance of filling it. And lastly, I am filled with gratitude for my precious wife Danielle, who provided love, support, friendship, and encouragement, served as a sounding board, and shouldered more than her share of the day-to-day tasks so that I may have the protected time needed to devote to this book. I am so grateful to God for raising up such a godly and enjoyable team to produce *Oaks in Office* for His glory and purposes. A heartfelt thanks to each of you!

RALPH DROLLINGER

INTRODUCTION

During my college basketball days at UCLA I experienced a strong calling into ministry. So strong was the calling that I decided to preach the Gospel with a Christian basketball team, Athletes in Action (AIA), rather than play professional basketball in the NBA. For the next four years I traveled the world with AIA, playing other national teams and preaching the Gospel at the halftimes. After that I continued in sports ministry, leading the umbrella group for all of America's sports ministries at the time, Sports Outreach America.

From the vantage point afforded me by those ministry opportunities I experienced the very fabric of the American sports ministry movement. I could see that the tremendous number of athletes living for Christ and talking openly in the media about their faith was directly related to the number of full-time sports ministers God raised up to disciple athletes. These were disciple-making, Bible-teaching evangelists who were on the campuses of high schools and colleges, and closely affiliated with professional athletes. During those years I watched God raise up hundreds of sports ministers throughout America, who in turn were fueling the conversion and spiritual growth of thousands of athletes.

Those experiences and insights were what inspired my wife Danielle and me to found Capitol Ministries® in 1996. With a similar vision, we thought, why not place disciple-making, Bible-teaching evangelists on the campuses of political leaders as well? In fact, very few state capitols, city governments, or federal capitols around the world had full-time ministers who were intent on building Public Servants in Christ. Why not do the same amongst them as we had seen done successfully for athletes and coaches?

So off we went to Sacramento to start Capitol Ministries® in the California Capitol. In the last several decades we have expanded the ministry from there into many U.S. state capitols, Washington D.C., and foreign federal capitals throughout the world, all by God's grace.

At the very heart of all that growth are solid Bible-teaching materials that lead the Public Servant into a deeper walk of faith and a personal relationship with Jesus Christ. That is the purpose of *Oaks In Office:* to provide in-depth Bible studies with custom applications to the life of a public leader. *Oaks in Office* consists of fifty-two carefully selected Bible studies from the hundreds that I have written over the past twenty-one years, presented in such an order that progressive study will mature you in Christ and teach you a Biblical perspective—a Christian worldview—that you can apply as you serve Him through your career.

Part 1 lays a Biblical foundation for public service

Part 2 studies sound Biblical precepts

Part 3 provides a Biblical perspective on personal character issues

Part 4 investigates social problems through a Biblical lens

Part 5 examines Biblical ways to increase personal faith

Part 6 explores Biblical methods for persevering and succeeding in office

We at Capitol Ministries® are intent on finding and training solid disciple-making, Bible-teaching evangelists to take the Gospel to their leaders in all of the capitals of the world. But that endeavor will only make disciples to the degree that sound doctrine is taught. *Oaks in Office* is designed to address that need, to challenge and mature Christian Public Servants who are just starting their Christian walk, as well as those who are mature in their faith. *"So faith comes from hearing, and hearing by the word of Christ,"* states Romans 10:17.

We encourage you to gather with other Public Servants in a small group and meet weekly to tackle each study together. Read *Oaks in Office* with a pencil in hand, so that you can interact with the text. The interaction among those in your group will prove most helpful, as we have found in our Bible studies with Members of the White House Cabinet, U.S. Senate, and House of Representatives in Washington, D.C. Embark on the journey with us and let us all grow in Christ together!

Now more than ever we need godly Public Servants. You have a privilege to have been called as one, but also a responsibility to represent the God of the Bible according to His Word. As you mature in Him, watch what God will accomplish in and through your life in the year ahead! Romans 12:1–2 urges us to be *"transformed by the renewing"* of our minds. May God transform and bless you as you become an Oak in Office!

AN OAK TREE'S ROOTS PUSH AS DEEP INTO THE EARTH as its branches reach toward the heavens. The oak tree's strength and endurance are due in great part to the network of strong and healthy roots that it spends the majority of time and energy building when it is young. The oak tree begins its life by shooting a taproot deeply into the ground to find a dependable source of moisture. After the taproot is stable and secure, the oak celebrates in foliage and branch growth. It continues to fortify its foundation as the years pass, growing an elaborate and extensive root system. Spreading horizontally beneath the ground up to seven times the width of its crown, these sturdy and durable roots will bring the tree moisture and nutrients all its life. This stable foundation also anchors the oak, enabling it to stand unyielding amid buffeting winds, assailing storms, and lightning strikes that easily topple weaker trees.

PART I

BUILDING A SCRIPTURAL FOUNDATION FOR EFFECTIVE PUBLIC SERVICE

"And you will even be brought before governors and kings for My sake, as a testimony to them …"

MATTHEW 10:18

CHAPTER 1

The Missing Mandate in Modern Missions

The foremost need of Public Servants is to know Christ. This is why Capitol Ministries® is focused on changing hearts by sharing the Gospel. Good legislation is important, but men and women can hardly be expected to make policies in accordance with sound, Biblically based principles if they are at odds with the author of Scripture. Only the Gospel has the power to change a heart. We believe that the objective of evangelizing and discipling political leaders is of the highest importance in the Capital Community. We need more disciplers!

Is there a Biblical basis for a calling to minister to political leaders? If so, how important is this in the mind of God? The answer is that Biblical evidence for modern missions to Public Servants runs through the whole Bible. Let's examine the supporting passages and help you to build a conviction regarding it.

The best way to reach other Public Servants with the Gospel of Jesus Christ is through evangelistic efforts. As a Public Servant, this should be of great interest to you! In that political leaders are essential to the Great Commission, it follows that you should be involved in its fulfillment! So let's explore the Biblical mandate to reach political leaders with the Gospel of Jesus Christ.

Exploring the Mandate

The following three passages from the New Testament provide the best initial understanding of the missiological emphasis as it touches on political leaders, which runs throughout the Word of God.

First Timothy 2:1–4

> *First of all, then, I urge that entreaties and prayers, petitions and thanksgivings, be made on behalf of all men, for kings and all who are in authority, so that we may lead a tranquil and quiet life in all godliness and dignity. This is good and acceptable in the sight of God our Savior, who desires all men to be saved and to come to the knowledge of the truth.*

The apostle Paul urges Timothy to pray evangelistically, not only for all people in general, but specifically for "*kings and all who are in authority.*" Very importantly, verse 1 begins, "*I urge.*" These words come from the original Greek *parakaleo*, which is a compound word comprised of the preposition *para* and the verb *kaleo*. *Para* means "alongside," while *kaleo* means "to call." Put together, *parakaleo* is an emphatic verb that means "to call to one's side." It is in the first-person singular: "*I urge* [you Timothy]."

Paul heightens this command with the words, "*first of all,*" or *protos* in the Greek, to indicate its priority (*protos* signifies preeminence rather than sequence). In other words, Paul wants Timothy to make it a priority to pray evangelistically for kings and those in authority. You'll notice a confirmation of the intent of this urging in the last portion of this passage, where it says that God "*desires all men to be saved and to come to the knowledge of the truth.*"

What we see here is not an afterthought in Paul's mind. Concern for political leaders is an emphasis that runs throughout his ministry, having been born at his Damascus road conversion. Notice these words of Jesus Himself in Acts 9:15:

Acts 9:15

> *"Go, for he* [Paul] *is a chosen instrument of Mine, to bear My name before the Gentiles and kings and the sons of Israel."*

Here Jesus reveals to His messenger Ananias that Paul (at that time known as Saul) is His *chosen instrument*. From the very outset of his calling Paul is *"to bear My* [Jesus'] *name before the Gentiles and kings and the sons of Israel."*

Kings are one of the specific groups that God calls Paul to evangelize.

There were many cities in the Roman Empire that had not heard the Gospel. So, the question might be asked, how did Paul decide where to travel? Certainly, there were many factors he considered, but one of those was the presence of political leaders. You will see below that his calling informed him regarding which cities he would go to in order to establish churches. It is very important to understand that the majority of cities Paul chose to visit were chosen in response to his Acts 9:15 calling. Note that many of those cities were capital cities in the Roman Empire:

- Paphos was the capital city of Cyprus
- Perga was the capital city of Pamphilia
- Pisidia Antioch was the capital city of So. Galatia
- Iconium was the capital city of Lyconia
- Thessalonica was the capital city of Macedonia
- Athens was a leading city of Greece
- Corinth was the capital city of Achaia
- Ephesus was the capital city of proconsular Asia

Paul ministered to both Jews and Gentiles, but among the Gentiles, Paul was specifically called to evangelize kings. That's why he went to these leading cities, as we shall see now.

The Book of Acts

Of the thirteen conversions recorded by Luke in the book of Acts, seven are politically related people.

This emphasis of reaching governing leaders is vividly illustrated in the third of our New Testament passages, the entire twenty-eight-chapter narrative of the book of Acts. It is insightful to note that Luke wrote both his Gospel account and the book of Acts to someone by the name of Theophilus (Luke 1:3; Acts 1:1). In that he calls him *most excellent*, a title used to address governors (Acts 23:26; 24:3; 26:25), it is quite possible that Luke wrote for the purpose of persuading a government leader to come to faith in Christ. This would explain why over half of the individual conversion accounts recorded in the book of Acts involve political figures. Luke's purpose could be either to relate to Theophilus that other government leaders have come to Christ, or to illustrate the fulfillment of Paul's call in Acts 9:15, if not both. Note the vocations of the following Acts converts:

- The Ethiopian eunuch was the treasurer of Candace, queen of the Ethiopians (Acts 8:27)
- Cornelius the centurion was a military leader (Acts 10:1)
- Blastus was the king's chamberlain (Acts 12:20)
- Sergius Paulus was a Roman provincial governor (proconsul) (Acts 13:7)
- The Philippian jailer was a keeper of prisoners (Acts 16:27–33)
- Dionysius was the Areopagite judge (Acts 17:34)
- Publius was the governor of Malta (Acts 28:7–8)

Paul's Acts 9:15 calling gives insight into why he desired to visit Rome and subsequently even travel as far as Spain. In Acts 23:11 the Lord reveals to Paul that he must testify of Him in Rome:

"Take courage; for as you have solemnly witnessed to My cause at Jerusalem, so you must witness at Rome also."

The apostle longs to fellowship with the church in Rome (Romans 1:10–12), but he has at least one other reason for making the voyage: evangelism. This is evident from Acts 27:24, where the Lord adds that Paul *"must stand before Caesar."* Therefore, out of obedience to his calling, Paul is compelled to take the Gospel to Caesar. History shows that

Caesar did not receive Christ, but Philippians 4:22 indicates that Paul's efforts are not in vain, as he is used by God in a powerful way amongst those in the emperor's palace:

All the saints greet you, especially those of Caesar's household.

Paul is a man governed by the vivid memory of his conversion as recorded in Acts 9, and specifically his calling to reach the leaders of the world with the Gospel. This consuming evangelistic zeal encompasses Paul's life after his Damascus road experience. His mission to Spain is aligned with that calling. Spain was a mineral-rich colony on the westernmost edge of the Empire. It had a population of Jews and Gentiles who hadn't heard the Gospel. Did Spain have a contingency of political leaders? Yes. The orator Quintilian, the writer Martial, and the statesman Seneca resided there. The Roman emperors Trajan and Hadrian were born there as well. Clement of Rome (writing in AD 95), speaks of a time when Paul had reached Spain and "had borne his testimony before the rulers."[1]

The apostle labored to reach political leaders with the Gospel throughout his years of ministry. His deep concern for their salvation perhaps explains why he gave such an emphatic mandate to Timothy in 1 Timothy 2:1–4, as we read above. There Paul instructs Timothy to pray for the salvation of Rome's political leaders. From Genesis to Revelation, God's people pursue evangelistic ministry to political leaders in foreign nations, and the same principle applies to believers today. Christians should desire to see their political leaders come to know Christ. In fact:

As a political leader, you are uniquely qualified to follow Paul's calling.

Expanding the Mandate

In addition to the apostle Paul, the apostle Peter also exemplified this emphasis of ministry in the New Testament. Moving forward from the church age, tribulation saints will have a ministry to unbelieving kings.

Looking the other way in the Bible, back toward the Old Testament nation of Israel, we find that God's chosen people were to be representatives of God's glory, shining forth His holiness to the Gentile nations of the world. And even more specifically, the nation Israel was to testify of God to political leaders in those Gentile nations. We will see this in some select passages that follow.

The ministry of reaching political leaders runs throughout all of Scripture. One of God's choice servants says in this regard, "*I will also speak of Your testimonies before kings And shall not be ashamed*" (Psalm 119:46).

Exemplifying the Mandate

The proposition that there is a missing mandate in modern missions today—that of reaching political leaders as a first priority—can be supported by looking at prior Biblical epochs when that mandate was operative. Bible history points to an historical thread of emphasis near to the heart of God that is woefully underemphasized in today's Christian missiology.

THE MINISTRY OF OLD TESTAMENT ISRAEL

God promises Abraham he will one day receive land, have numerous descendants, and be blessed by God (Genesis 12:1–3). Four centuries pass as Abraham's descendants grow from one family into twelve tribes and finally into the nation Israel. The Lord calls them out of the world to be His "*own possession,*" "*a kingdom of priests and a holy nation*" (Exodus 19:5–6). Israel is called to demonstrate the holiness of God to all the surrounding nations.

God intends for His people to be a light to the Gentile nations in a general sense, and more specifically He expects His people to be a light to the leaders of those nations. Isaiah 60:3 tells us in this regard:

> "*Nations will come to your light, And kings to the brightness of your rising.*"

Isaiah 62:1–2 suggests the same type of ministry for Israel. The Lord expects Gentile leaders to take notice of His chosen people, a nation set apart for His purposes. One illustration of Israel's fulfillment of God's calling to reach political leaders is the Queen of Sheba, when she visits Israel during the reign of Solomon (1 Kings 10:1–10). The queen travels a distance of fourteen hundred miles to see the splendorous city of Jerusalem, and she does not leave disappointed. First Kings 10:5 (ESV) says that as a result of the visit, "*there was no more breath in her,*" which is an OT euphemism similar to our current expression, "She was simply blown away!" The queen is overwhelmed, and proceeds to praise the Lord (1 Kings 10:9). The words of Jesus in Luke 11:31 imply that during this time the queen is converted. Solomon's testimony and the testimony of God's blessings on Israel at that time prove compelling in evangelizing this foreign leader.

A second illustration of Israel's obedience to her calling to reach political leaders from Gentile nations occurs when Solomon finishes the temple. He gives thanks to God. During his thanksgiving prayer he reminds Israel that the

Lord has blessed them for a purpose: "*so that all the peoples of the earth may know that the Lord is God; there is no one else*" (1 Kings 8:60). The temple itself even includes a court for the Gentiles to worship the God of Israel. As the nations see Israel's light, the hope is that, like the Queen of Sheba, they will come from afar, led by their kings, to worship the God of Israel. God wants Israel to be magnetically attractive to Gentile nations and their leaders. States Isaiah 60:11 in this regard:

> "*Your gates will be open continually; They will not be closed day or night, So that men may bring to you the wealth of the nations, With their kings led in procession.*"

The ministry of Old Testament Israel is further illustrated in yet another way by the prophetic ministry of Jonah. Though a reluctant Jewish minister, Jonah eventually goes (in a "whale" of a roundabout way) to the Gentile city of Nineveh and calls upon its citizens to repent of their wickedness. Many listen, and soon Jonah has the opportunity to call the king to repentance. The king responds to the call to repentance and orders the entire city to follow suit, as we read in a very profound passage of Scripture (Jonah 3:3–10).

As illustrated by these three passages, Israel possessed a great calling to shine forth to the nations of the world with God's glory, and an important aspect of that was to reach the leaders of those nations.

THE MINISTRY OF JESUS AND THE DISCIPLES

Jesus sends out His disciples with a charge to evangelize political leaders. When He commissions the twelve, He tells them they will be "*brought before governors and kings for My sake, as a testimony to them*" (Matthew 10:18).

THE MINISTRY OF THE APOSTLES

As a crescendo to the various politically related conversions in the book of Acts, Paul seeks to minister to Caesar and his household by visiting Rome. And even beyond that He desires to visit Spain to preach the Gospel to leaders residing there (Romans 15:23–24). Therefore Paul's charges to Timothy (1 Timothy 2:1–4), as previously noted, and to Titus in Titus 3:1 underscore the importance of carrying forth this mandate today in the church age.

Paul is not the only apostle imbued with a passion to minister to kings; Peter has the same aspirations, albeit not evidenced quite as directly.

In 1 Peter 2:12, Peter exhorts his audience to live exemplary lives amongst the Gentiles for one purpose: that they may "*glorify God in the day of visitation.*" This is his way of saying that he desires for Gentiles they come into contact with to come to know Christ. He knows that poor conduct in the church will lead to a poor testimony in the community. Interestingly, verses 13 and 14 of 1 Peter 2 expand upon this idea with respect specifically to political leaders. Simply stated, evangelism to Gentile kings and governors will only be effective to the extent that believers humbly submit themselves to those leaders and the laws they enact (so long as they are not unbiblical of course). So when we read 1 Peter 2:13–14 we must remember that it is set in the context of being a good witness to leaders:

> *Submit yourself for the Lord's sake to every human institution, whether to a king as the one in authority, or to governors as sent by him …*

THE MINISTRY OF TRIBULATION SAINTS

During the Olivet Discourse in Mark 13, Jesus teaches on events that will unfold during the tribulation. Wars will erupt, natural disasters will occur, and persecution will be common for Christ's followers. Mark 13:9 concludes this description by adding:

> *"But be on your guard; for they will deliver you to the courts, and you will be flogged in the synagogues, and you will stand before governors and kings for My sake, as a testimony to them."*

I believe that followers of Christ will be raptured before this prophecy is fulfilled, and that it is those who come to Christ during the tribulation who are being spoken of here. They will be witnesses to governing leaders *for Jesus' sake*. It is noteworthy that amongst the limited details Jesus provides regarding the tribulation, he makes specific mention of evangelizing political leaders. Mark 13:9 states that believers "*will stand before governors and kings for My sake, as a testimony to them.*" Thus, the thread of ministry to those in the political arena will continue even during this future epoch of great upheaval.

THE MINISTRY OF MILLENNIAL SAINTS

Subsequent to Christ's second coming, God's people will no longer minister to kings, for they will become kings themselves (2 Timothy 2:12; Revelation 5:10; 20:4, 6). Those who have been redeemed will be given the privilege of helping rule on earth. When Christ returns and His kingdom has come, He will grant believers governing positions similar to those held today. Believers will then rule with perfection under the authority of "*the King of kings.*" The perfect future political leadership of Christ and His called-out ones is impossible to achieve in today's fallen world. Praise God for that future day! The type of ministry will change from one of pursuing to one of being, but God's keen interest in government leaders will nonetheless remain intact even during the millennial kingdom.

Engaging the Mandate

The Great Commission includes the specific strategic element of emphasis on reaching political leaders throughout the world with the Gospel of Jesus Christ. This insight becomes quite evident from the passages examined in this chapter. Capitol Ministries® is a missional response to this mandate. We welcome your partnership in this God-ordained calling! Are you pursuing what is foremost in importance—*protos*—in the fulfillment of the Great Commission?

Has this brief exploration caused you to begin to question whether missions to political leaders should remain a "missing mandate" of evangelism? With all the confusion about Church and State, perhaps you've always wondered if it is even appropriate for believers to be involved in politics at all. Rather than allow that uncertainty to undermine you, let's face the question head-on, as we embark together on this journey of Biblical discovery.

Notes

1 John Chapman, "Pope Clement the First," *Early Christian Writings*, accessed October 12, 2017, http://www.earlychristianwritings.com/info/1clement-cathen.html.

"You are the salt of the earth; but if the salt has become tasteless, how can it be made salty again? It is no longer good for anything, except to be thrown out and trampled underfoot by men. You are the light of the world. A city set on a hill cannot be hidden; nor does anyone light a lamp and put it under a basket, but on the lampstand, and it gives light to all who are in the house. Let your light shine before men in such a way that they may see your good works, and glorify your Father who is in heaven."

MATTHEW 5:13–16

CHAPTER 2

Should Believers Be Involved in Politics?

What a privilege it is for me to bring you, our nation's Public Servants, my insights on the Christian walk as it relates to your life in government, gleaned from the Word of God, the Bible. We will touch on both the personal application of the truths found in God's Word, and the application that has an eye toward public policy and the national effects of following, and not following, God's Word. We embark on our journey with a few assumptions: Firstly, that God's Word is the final word on what is best for us as individuals and in the governance of our nation. Secondly, we proceed on the assumption that government is a proper place for believers to function in society. Some may not agree with this second assumption. For that reason, we begin by addressing this concern. Should believers in Jesus restrict themselves to personal evangelism, and stay out of government?

I used to be in the camp that argues against political involvement by believers, but that began to change some years ago when I personally witnessed the leading advocate of this position, a megachurch pastor in Southern California, rally his congregation to attend and show support en masse at a city council meeting. At that meeting the decision would be made as to whether the Christian college where he was president would be granted a land-use permit to construct a memorial chapel in his name. This glaring incongruity coalesced with my growing realization that I could not minister to believers in the California Capitol building if deep down I believed they were out of step with God's will by being involved in the political process. Those experiences opened me up to thinking through to the other side of this debate and to studying the Word on this matter with less of a predisposition.

Today I come down on the side that believers *are* to be involved in politics rather than isolated from it. In short, if every believer adhered to this somewhat popular evangelical teaching against political involvement, there would be no believers in office! There would be no *salt* and *light* influence in a representative form of government. What follows are the Biblical arguments for participation in the governance of the State in ways beyond personal evangelism.

The fact that believers should affect the world in which they live rather than isolate themselves from it is evident from the Sermon on the Mount. Note Matthew 5:13–16:

> *"You are the salt of the earth; but if the salt has become tasteless, how can it be made salty again? It is no longer good for anything, except to be thrown out and trampled under foot by men. You are the light of the world. A city set on a hill cannot be hidden; nor does anyone light a lamp and put it under a basket, but on the lampstand, and it gives light to all who are in the house. Let your light shine before men in such a way that they may see your good works, and glorify your Father who is in heaven."*

When Jesus lights a lamp—that is, when He brings an individual to true saving faith in Himself—what results is a person who *"gives light to all who are in the house."*[1] This is not difficult to decipher from this passage. The word *house* (v. 15) is another way of expressing two previously used words in the passage. This simply means a believer will affect people on the *earth* (v. 13a), and people in the *world* (v. 14a). This passage teaches that it is normal for believers to influence the physical *earth/world*, or the land in which they live.

Notice the progression of this passage: verses 13–16 come after verses 1–12 of Matthew 5, which are commonly known as Jesus' Beatitudes. The Beatitudes teach concise virtues (listed in the opening portion of His Sermon on the Mount) that are characteristic of His mature followers: *gentleness* (v. 5), *righteousness* (vv. 6, 10), *mercifulness* (v. 7), *purity* (v. 8), etc. Recognizing the progressive nature of this passage, we see that our ability to be salt and light—expressing the idea that believers are to be preservers and illuminators in the earth/world—is founded on these virtues. The point is that we cannot affect our surroundings in a godly way unless we first possess godly character.

How we affect the world is intrinsically linked to who we are.

Such an interpretation of the meaning of this passage is supported by the following key grammatical understandings: firstly, the twice-used verb at the beginning of verses 13 and 14 is "you are" (*humeis este*). This verb is present active indicative in the Greek language, in contrast to imperative. This is a subtle but important distinction. It means *we are* Christ-influencing in culture—agents of the preservation and illumination of truth—to the degree that we are mature in Christ. Jesus is not saying, "I command you to be salt and light!" Rather, He is teaching that when you manifest Christlikeness, you affect your world, or in the case of the Capital Community, its people and its laws. In other words, Jesus is saying, "*you are* preserving and illuminating society to the degree that you are *beatitudinal!*" If we seek to be beatitudinal, always connected to Christlike maturity—we preserve and illuminate the world!

Secondly, notice the beginning of the next verse, verse 16, in the original language. The adverb at the start of the passage further supports the idea of Jesus' sequential thinking relative to what He has previously delineated. "*Let your light shine before men in such a way.*" "In such a way" (*houtos*) means "in this way," or "thus." That is, our light is to shine according to what has already been said. Here the verb "shine" (*lampo*) is in the imperative, meaning God is commanding you. In other words, our *light* must *shine* in this way. And what is this *way*? That others *see* our godly character and the resulting preservation and illumination in the world. What results is that others "*glorify your Father who is in heaven.*" That is to say, by following this formula you can become a powerful witness in a fallen world! Here is a summation:

Spiritual Maturation	Cultural Participation	World Evangelization
(Matthew 5:1–12)	(Matthew 5:13–15)	(Matthew 5:16)

Personal spiritual maturity will be followed by cultural participation, which then testifies of God to an onlooking world. This progression reveals the Biblical formula for effective testimony—for glorifying God in a fallen world.

To those who say that the believer should only be about evangelism, this passage speaks to their omission of a vital and necessary step: cultural participation in the world is essential to becoming an effective witness!

Can an evangelist who shuns cultural involvement be effective?[2] The idea that one should be all about evangelism without cultural engagement is an unbiblical misconception. Matthew 5 does not support that idea; Jesus Himself does not support it. This passage lends to correcting such thinking. One cannot bypass the need for evangelists to be preservers and illuminators within the context of their culture—that is, in the world.

And if this argument is insufficient, what follows are additional Biblically supported reasons why believers should be involved in politics.

Evangelism alone is too narrow an understanding of the mission of Jesus.

In the Great Commission of Matthew 28:19–20 Jesus commands His followers to do more than just teach others the Gospel, as important as that is. He commands believers to go beyond evangelism and "*make disciples.*" How is the believer to do that? By "*teaching* [others] *to observe all that I commanded you.*" Paul echoes this when he says to the Ephesian elders, "*For I did not shrink from declaring to you the whole purpose of God*" (Acts 20:27). Paul says regarding all of his writings, "*The things which I write to you are the Lord's commandment*" (1 Corinthians 14:37). Peter says regarding his *beyond-salvation* teachings: "*that you should remember … the commandment of the Lord and Savior spoken by your apostles*" (2 Peter 3:2). Jesus wants others to know *all* of His instruction. That means He wants His followers to learn about marriage, family, church, commerce, and government. This is required to make disciples. While the primary objective of Jesus' mission is to convert the lost, the entirety of His message encompasses making disciples.

The notion that the believer should only evangelize political leaders and not get involved in politics represents myopic thinking. It follows from this idea that evangelists would need to counsel their Public-Servant converts to immediately leave office, and if every elected leader were won to Christ the government would have to shut down!

So, what does Jesus teach—what is "*the whole counsel of God*" (Acts 20:27 NKJV)—regarding civil government? Among other things it is this: He Himself created it (Genesis 1:26; Colossians 1:16); He ordained it (Romans 13:1); He sustains it (Colossians 1:17); and it is intended to restrain a fallen world (Romans 13:4). In addition to His saving grace, Jesus' purposes, compelled by a heart of compassion for the lost (Matthew 9:36), manifest common grace and restraining grace to all of His creation (Matthew 5:45b) through this ordained institution. How great is His love!

Jesus has a purpose for the institution of government besides evangelism. One of the leading advocates for the "evangelism, not politics" viewpoint states:

[Jesus] did not come to earth to make the old creation moral through social and governmental reform but to make new creatures (His people) holy through the saving power of the gospel and the transforming work of the Holy Spirit.[3]

He is propagating too narrow an understanding of the mission of Jesus! This does not represent the whole counsel of God because it does not acknowledge His purposes for His institution of civil government. As important as evangelism is, in government as elsewhere, there must always be the broader understanding of Jesus' teachings regarding government. The believer must also be about teaching what Scripture says about civil government and more specifically, teaching these truths to civil government leaders!

Another error of this same influential Christian author is his tendency to spiritualize away the importance of good civil government in the propagation of the Gospel. He states:

The ideal human government can ultimately do nothing to advance God's kingdom, and the worst, most despotic worldly government in the end cannot halt the power of the Holy Spirit or the spread of God's Word.[4]

In an ultimate sense, in view of the sovereignty of God what is said here is true. But is this a tenable argument for non-involvement in civil government by believers? One does not have to be much of a student of current geopolitics, world history, or historic missions to know that Middle Eastern countries, North Korea, Cuba, and Russia, among others, have suppressed the growth of the Body of Christ to a much greater degree than other countries. How many missionaries have come forth from the aforementioned lands? Practically speaking, why have 90 percent of world missions in the past century been funded by America? Shouldn't believers be involved in politics if for no other reason than to promote the spreading of God's Word? The nation that sends out missionaries can advance God's Kingdom.

Good government is important to the fulfillment of the Great Commission.

Countries that honor freedom make possible the pursuit of the Great Commission, as seen presently and in history. That means the believer's role in sustaining a country's health and well-being is noble and important, and is in keeping with what Jesus commanded us.

To illustrate one of many possible results of living by too narrow an understanding of the mission of Jesus, consider that radio preachers must now edit their radio broadcasts in Canada so as to not include any mention of Romans 1. This is due to new Canadian laws introduced by non-Christians. This life-changing book addresses the severity of sin, the principle of justification, the importance of faith, the ministry of the Holy Spirit, and the gifts of the Spirit, among other major issues of faith. What will become of the great radio ministries in the U.S. that have so affected our culture for good and evangelized to the lost if our laws, devoid of Christian influence, also begin to limit our freedoms?[5] Government can indeed facilitate or hinder the advance of God's kingdom.

Shouldn't believers be involved in civil government if only for the sake of the Great Commission? Indeed, church leaders should applaud, respect, support, sustain, prepare, and elect more Christian political leaders to, among other things, preserve the leaders' freedom to propagate the Gospel. Christian Legislators that I know view themselves in a partnership with pastors. In turn, pastors should view themselves in partnership with Christian Legislators.

Should the Church raise up young men and women to run for office with the same passion and enthusiasm that it places on raising up godly pastors, wives, husbands, children, and businessmen? Absolutely, yes!

The mission of Jesus includes the transformation of society.

If "*teaching them to observe all that I commanded you*" is central to the Great Commission as the starting point for making disciples,[6] then the mission of Jesus has an eye toward the transformation of marriages, families, commerce, and governments. The mission of Jesus has a sum total intent of transforming society as a whole, or as it is called in the Great Commission passage, *nations* (*ethnos*). Believers are to affect nations! Those who advocate too narrow a view of Jesus' mission are forced to interpret *ethnos* to mean "people groups" so as to comport the passage to their viewpoint of non-involvement in civil government. But for those who hold a bigger view of Jesus' mission, while individual evangelism is inescapable, so is affecting nations for good.

Which parts of the Bible should *not* be preached about?

The pastor or teacher who holds to "evangelism, not politics" has a limited understanding of Jesus' mission, and to support this view must omit certain portions of the Bible, such as Genesis 9:5–6, John 19:11, Acts 25:11, Romans 13:1–7, or 1 Peter 2:13–14. Those passages all have to do with believers relating to government. Does one avoid teaching about Joseph's influence on Pharaoh's government, or Daniel's influence on Nebuchadnezzar's government? By way of extension, if one "just preaches the Gospel," should one avoid teaching on marriage and family? What parts of the whole counsel of God should the Bible teacher omit? This leads to a huge incongruity in light of 2 Timothy 3:16–17, which says, "*All Scripture is inspired by God and profitable for teaching*," and Acts 20:27, which says, "*declaring to you the whole purpose of God.*"

God leaves Christians here on earth both for evangelism and to do good for others.

God tends to leave His saints on earth after He saves them. After they are saved, what are believers to do? Should they only evangelize others for the remainder of their earthly life? What about Matthew 22:39: "*You shall love your neighbor as yourself*"? This command is listed six other times in the New Testament. Like the Great Commission command, this is a command from Jesus as well! The spirit of this command demands that we consider the following kinds of issues: making sure the law punishes thieves who rob my neighbors; working to create and enforce laws pertaining to internet privacy to protect my neighbors from hackers who would steal their credit card information; promoting policies that ensure that those who educate my neighbors' children cannot teach them things that are evil. How could these endeavors that are completely compatible with the mandates of Scripture be accomplished if not by Christians involved in policy making? One could argue that there is a strong Biblical connection between loving our neighbor and being involved in civil government. Galatians 6:10 tells believers, "*So then, while we have opportunity, let us do good to all people, and especially to those who are of the household of the faith.*" Ephesians 2:10 further cites societal responsibility when it says, "*For we are His workmanship, created in Christ Jesus for good works, which God prepared beforehand so that we would walk in them.*" In the words of Wayne Grudem, "Why should churches teach their people how to do good works in hospitals and in schools, and in businesses and in neighborhoods, but not in government?"[7]

God established both Church and State to restrain evil.

When a person comes to Christ, the work of the Holy Spirit causes internal regeneration that quells evil in that person's heart (2 Corinthians 5:17). However, history and present observation indicate that not everyone comes to Christ, nor are converts completely and immediately sanctified. Therefore, in addition to the Church, God has instituted civil government to restrain evil by the use of force and punishment in a fallen world. Romans 13:4 is clear about this where Paul states, speaking of government, "*but if you do what is evil, be afraid; for it does not bear the sword for nothing; for it is a minister of God, an avenger who brings wrath on the one who practices evil.*" 1 Peter 2:13–14 states similarly, "*Submit yourselves … to every human institution, whether to a king as the one in authority, or to governors as sent by him for the punishment of evildoers.*"[8] God vests His authority in civil government (Romans 13:1) in order to restrain evil in a fallen world. Whereas the Church is God's conduit of saving grace, the State is God's conduit of restraining grace. Such a realization necessitates the believer's involvement in civil government, since it is part of Jesus' overall mission.

One other point is worthy of mention here. Christian isolationists often harbor ideological superiority: as if the authority of the Church is over the authority of the State. The Church is not over the State; the Church must submit to the State. The glaringly embarrassing American historical illustration of this is the Emancipation Proclamation of 1863. The abolition of slavery came not from the institution of the Church via evangelism. It was the State that birthed a human being's freedom from another person's ownership. Sometimes the State restrains evil more effectively than the Church!

As another example, it was not the punctuality of church leaders that gave us the canonization of the New Testament. It wasn't until the Roman Emperor Constantine in the early fourth century demanded it from Eusebius that the Church got around to sewing the twenty-seven books together! Believers should respect the unique role of the State and not carry a condescending attitude toward it.

> Let us not shrink from involvement in civil government, lest we
> end up inheriting a lawless country and lose our religious freedoms.

Christians have positively influenced the State throughout history.

Let's look at three ways in which believers have influenced the State through history. Accounts are numerous and well documented by authors Schmidt[9] and Colson[10] in their wonderful works. Here is a summary:

THE DIGNITY OF MANKIND

The historic spread of Christian influence on the State has been responsible for many victories: the outlawing of infanticide, child abandonment, and abortion in the Roman Empire (AD 374); prohibition of the burning alive of widows in India (1829); ending slavery in the British Empire (1840); the ending of binding of women's feet in China (1912); the outlawing of racial discrimination in America. These are but a few of the historic contributions of Christians engaged in politics.

THE CONSTITUTIONS OF MANKIND

Christians were influential in the writing of the Magna Carta in England in 1215, the Declaration of Independence in America in 1776, and the Constitution of the United States in 1787. These are the most important documents in the history of governments. All these documents were significantly influenced by believers and are the basis not only of prosperous countries, but of the Christian mission movement worldwide. The advanced views of government spelled out in these documents have birthed individual freedoms, justice, freedom of religion, and the separation of Church and State.

THE EDUCATION OF MANKIND

Believers have greatly influenced the development of higher education in America. Of the 182 colleges and universities in America in 1932, 92 percent had been founded by Christian denominations. Such influence has led to the advancement of a society heretofore unknown in world history, a society that has accelerated the Great Commission to levels of accomplishment equal to that of the first century Church.

These are but a few illustrations of Christian influence on the State. Therefore, when a prominent Christian author reasons in 2000, "God does not call the church to influence the culture by promoting legislation and court rulings that advance a scriptural point of view," and "Using temporal methods to promote legislative and judicial change … is not our calling—and has no eternal value,"[11] one wonders how he can arrive at such a narrow understanding of the mission of Jesus. In his commentary on Matthew 5:13–16 dating back to 1985 this author said, "Christians can have a powerful influence on the welfare of the world."[12] And therein he quotes Martyn Lloyd-Jones who said, "[What saved England was that] … [t]he political situation was affected, and the great Acts of Parliament which were passed in the last century were mostly due to the fact that there were such large numbers of individual Christians found in the land."[13] Unfortunately, in the year 2000, this same writer wrote a book to attempt to influence pastors to avoid governmental involvement (see fn3). History, as well as the argument of Matthew 5:1–16, favors this author's more Biblical 1985 position.

Doesn't the Bible say that persecution is coming?

When studying eschatology, the study of future Biblical events, one could reason that since things are going to get worse in the end times (see Matthew 24:9–12; 21–22; 2 Timothy 3:1–5) we may as well not attempt to improve government today. The response is simple: in the meantime, the believer is to be salt and light (Matthew 5:13–15); and we are to love our neighbor (Matthew 22:39), and do good works (Ephesians 2:10), in addition to evangelizing the lost (Matthew 5:16). One cannot disobey the clear commands of God in the here and now in lieu of end-time passages. A fatalistic view of the future of the world is no excuse for failure to act in the present moment. Scripture explicitly mentions that no one knows the exact time of Christ's second coming (Matthew 24:36; 25:13), therefore believers should influence civil government for good as long as they are able.

Could political involvement distract believers from the main task of preaching the Gospel?

If indeed God has called the believer to be salt and light as a basis for evangelism, the question isn't whether political involvement by the Church will divert energy away from preaching the Gospel. The question is about how we can come to understand political involvement as a means of expanding opportunities for preaching the Gospel.

Believers should be involved in politics in ways similar to their involvement in making their marriage better, their family better, their business better, or their church better. Running for office and serving in civil government is no less spiritual than going into full-time ministry.

Having established that believers do indeed belong in government, let us now look at how you can be most effective in impacting the world through public service.

Notes

1 "Gives light" is a present active indicative verb.

2 In 1 Corinthians 9:22b the apostle Paul states, "I have become all things to all men, so that I may by all means save some." This is an appropriate supporting passage for a Scriptural understanding of cultural involvement. Paul was willing to get involved in the lives, cultures, and professions of others (including the political arena, e.g., Philippians 1:13; 4:22; Acts 26:28ff.), without compromising Biblical truth, in order to evangelize the lost. How can today's Church evangelize politicians if it is unwilling to connect with politicians?

3 John MacArthur, *Why Government Can't Save You: An Alternative to Political Activism* (Grand Rapids: Zondervan, 2000), 11–12. It is worth noting MacArthur's exposition of Romans 13:1–7 in 1994 wherein he speaks about ordination and moralization: "Human government is ordained by God for the benefit of society…. In order to promote and protect the good in society human government must punish the evil." (John MacArthur, *The MacArthur New Testament Commentary: Romans 9–16* [Chicago: Moody, 1994], 218, 225.) Implicit in his comments is his seeming admission of a broader role of the mission of Jesus (see Colossians 1:16). Unfortunately, his later contradictory thinking ("evangelism, not politics") has influenced many.

4 Ibid., 7.

5 Many leading Christian thinkers believe one of the major reasons America has not gone the way of Europe is due to the presence and power of Christian radio.

6 It is noteworthy that Christ did not end His ministry commanding His followers to evangelize, but rather to make disciples.

7 Wayne Grudem, *Politics According to the Bible* (Grand Rapids: Zondervan, 2010), 48. Please note that I am utilizing Dr. Grudem's chapter outline (with its much-appreciated comprehensiveness) in this study with his permission.

8 The one exception to obedience to the authority of the State is when civil obedience would necessitate disobedience to God's Word (see Exodus 1:17; Daniel 3:16–18; 6:7, 10; Acts 4:19).

9 Alvin Schmidt, *How Christianity Changed the World* (Grand Rapids: Zondervan, 2004).

10 Charles Colson, *God and Government: An Insider's View on the Boundaries between Faith and Politics* (Grand Rapids: Zondervan, 2007). Previously published as *Kingdoms in Conflict*.

11 MacArthur, *Why Government Can't Save You*, 130, 15.

12 John MacArthur, *The MacArthur New Testament Commentary: Matthew 1–7* (Chicago: Moody Press, 1985), 243.

13 Martyn Lloyd-Jones, *Studies in the Sermon on the Mount* (Grand Rapids: Eerdmans, 1971), 1:157, (as quoted in John MacArthur, *Why Government Can't Save You.*

"You are the salt of the earth.... You are the light of the world.... Let your light shine."

MATTHEW 5:13–16

CHAPTER 3

How to Maximize Your Influence on the Hill

In the Sermon on the Mount Jesus states, "*You are the salt of the earth.... You are the light of the world.*" My desire is to provide you with a greater understanding of the Greek verb that Jesus uses: *you are*. As we discussed in chapter 1, it is not an imperative command; it is an indicative verb. This is a very important and necessary distinction to make as we seek to better understand what the Bible means by what it says. Such precision leads to proper, God-glorifying application to one's life.

My prayer is that the meaning of this passage will become increasingly clear as you study what follows.

In the three-chapter Sermon on the Mount (Matthew 5–7), Jesus denounces the legalism of the Pharisees, building the case that one cannot be saved by keeping the law of Moses. The Pharisees fashioned themselves as the astute spiritual gurus of Israel, habitually staking out the moral high ground (with their odious scent of superiority). Jesus' objective in the three-chapter sermon is in part to pop their bubble. He begins His sermon with pithy, short statements intended to contrast with their posturing. These Beatitudes (declarations of a specific condition for being blessed or gaining a kind of bliss) are all direct opposites of pharisaical arrogance and ideology. In other words, Jesus can be understood as saying to the Pharisees, "You think your ways will change the world? You've got it backwards!"

That summation of Jesus' sermon should give a hint as to how Public Servants can maximize their influence on the Hill. By the time you get to the conclusion of the Beatitudes (Matthew 7:13–14), the formula for an effective, God-honoring life that impacts the world has been laid out. When we read, "*You are the salt of the earth.... You are the light of the world*," the two "*You are*" statements serve as apt summaries of what we have come to call *beatitudinal* character in action!

Well-meaning believers often invoke this passage as a means of encouragement to prod others to step up to the plate and affect the world. But isolating Jesus' salt and light statements with no reference to what precedes them misses the crux of the passage. It is like expecting a staff member to achieve a certain function without instruction—speech writers must first know how to write; webmasters must first know HTML; schedulers must first master their software—to be effective in their vocations. Similarly, Public Servants must first know what will make them preservers and illuminators (salt and light, respectively) while serving in office. This point is simple yet profound: Jesus' statement about being salt and light is a codification of what He has taught just moments before in the Sermon on the Mount. The seven Beatitudes need be thoroughly examined and integrated in order to become salt and light. Let's begin that now.

Seven Required Attitudes: Matthew 5:1–9

> When Jesus saw the crowds, He went up on the mountain; and after He sat down, His disciples came to Him. He opened His mouth and began to teach them.

During the time of Christ there were four prevalent religious groups that focused on things other than the inner man that Jesus emphasizes—that is, one's attitudes. Notice these four groups and possible parallels to today:

THE RELIGIOUS GROUPS OF JESUS' DAY

- The **Pharisees** insisted on fastidious adherence to the Mosaic Law (and all that they had *added* to the Law).

- The **Sadducees** were akin to the theological liberalism of today. They discounted the supernatural, conforming everything to concepts within their reasoning abilities.

- The **Essenes** were ascetics, believing in dualism: the material world was seen as evil and to be avoided.

- The **Zealots** believed the end game of all religion was political activism. Theirs was a call to take up arms against Rome.

This was the competitive theological landscape wherein Jesus spoke of the following seven characteristics of the blessed—that is, those who are pleasing to self, God, and others. As we study these characteristics, pay special attention to the progression—how each builds on the former. There is a definite accumulation of thought here. That is to say, the Beatitudes which follow are not a buckshot scattering of somewhat unrelated, nice sayings; they are *"precept upon precept; line upon line"* (Isaiah 28:10 KJV).

1. IF YOU BREAK OVER PERSONAL SIN

"Blessed are the poor in spirit, for theirs is the kingdom of heaven." (Matthew 5:3)

The first necessary component for long-lasting influence and true spirituality in God's sight is humility. The Greek word Matthew selects, translated into English as "poor" (*ptochos*), was used in association with a beggar, connoting the idea of material poverty. Here Jesus uses it in a spiritual sense: being spiritually poor—one who is begging God for salvation. Foundational to our relationship to self, God, and others is the need to come to grips with our abject spiritual poverty—a realization of our lost hopelessness apart from God's intervention. Fundamental to effective influence is acknowledgement of God (versus self) and His divine enablement. This stands in opposition to the one who possesses a spirit of self-sufficiency, the seedbed of personal pride.

Paul reflects on this attitude in Philippians 3:7–9 when he describes his personal righteousness, in comparison to God's, as *rubbish*. Isaiah 64:6 puts it this way: *"And all our righteous deeds are like a filthy garment."* Though counterintuitive, worthiness in this world cannot be attained without a sense of personal unworthiness. We must take our eyes off of self and *"regard one another as more important than yourselves"* (Philippians 2:3). Without genuine humility others will rightfully conclude that we think "it's all about me," which vastly diminishes our influence. Such was the rap on the Pharisees. The *poor in spirit* (akin to being repentant) are *blessed* because after taking personal inventory they've recognized a need to depend on God for their salvation; Jesus concludes, "*theirs is the kingdom of heaven.*"

2. IF YOU MOURN OVER PERSONAL SIN

"*Blessed are those who mourn, for they shall be comforted.*" (Matthew 5:4)

The contextual progression of thought leading to "mourning" (*pentheo*) has to do with sorrowfulness over the personal sin that has broken us and brought us to an understanding of our poverty. It is a present participle meaning this outlook should be one of continuous action, reflective not only of personal repentance leading to salvation, but an ongoing attitude that "*nothing good dwells in me, that is, in my flesh*" (Romans 7:18). The person who is poor in spirit realizes his personal bankruptcy, which leads naturally to mourning, grief, and agony over one's plight before a Holy and righteous God. James underscores this perspective on self when he writes, "*Be miserable and mourn and weep; let your laughter be turned into mourning and your joy to gloom.*" (James 4:9). *Mourning*—that is, longing for a life free from sin and with one's Maker (cf. 2 Corinthians 5:2, 8)—implores God for His attention and empowerment: "*for they shall be comforted.*"

Contrary to the ways of the Pharisees, it is the emptying of self that enables the filling of God.

"*For when I am weak, then I am strong*" is a similarly counterintuitive paradox found in 2 Corinthians 12:10. It is spiritual bankruptcy (being poor in spirit), leading to personal continual mourning, which in turn facilitates Jesus' conclusion of this Beatitude. The word "comforted" (*parakaleo*), "to call to one's side" (cf. 2 Corinthians 1:3), is the same word used elsewhere for the Holy Spirit, which can be translated "Helper." Paraphrased: "Blessed are those who mourn, for they shall receive the help of God." Do you desire greater influence on the Hill? Here is the Biblical prescription: sober yourself to your abject personal spiritual poverty. Once you realize you're not so great, your very grief over your condition can position your for effective service; it is at this point God aids you.

Whereas the first two Beatitudes focus on one's proper assessment of self, the following two pertain to a proper assessment of oneself in relation to God.

3. IF YOU DESIRE GOD'S APPROVAL

"Blessed are the gentle, for they shall inherit the earth." (Matthew 5:5)

If by being poor in spirit and mourning over sin one has forsaken personal merit in exchange for God's gracious impartation, then it follows that one will possess a *gentle* spirit, in view of the holiness of God.

Gentleness, translated in some English Bibles as *meekness*, has as its object the awe and respect of God. It means *not self-strong*. The Greek word for "gentleness" (*praus*) carries the idea of focus on the holiness of God. Contextually then, this is not so much about being gentle with others; it is about being humbled in the presence of the reality of who God is! I am meek when I compare my sinfulness to God's holiness. In contrast, the Pharisees were full of hubris and depended on their personal merit. The redeemed are full of meekness in awe of God's majesty and holiness.

What results is that *"they shall inherit the earth."* In terms of being salt and light today, the quality of not being self-strong—that is, being desirous of God's approval—is an indispensable component for developing a God-given influence on the Hill.

4. IF YOU SEEK AFTER GOD'S WAYS

"Blessed are those who hunger and thirst for righteousness, for they shall be satisfied." (Matthew 5:6)

Having given oneself a vote of no confidence, one will not only be awestruck, i.e., meek in view of His holiness, but will also pursue, or *hunger and thirst*, after His *righteousness*. Void of self, one desires to be filled with God's ways! Show me a Member who hungers for God's righteousness and I will show you a Member who is effectuating change in society; the inverse is true also.

Hungering and thirsting connote a strong passion in the soul. Herein is proper ambition: not zeal to be famous or create a brand, but zeal to know God! The more one crucifies and empties self (Galatians 2:20) the more one will desire to be filled with God's ways. *We cannot grab hold of God's pearls until we release the pop-beads of self!*

This is the means of ultimate satisfaction in this life, and these are the foundational ingredients of those who will be effective agents of preservation and illumination in culture.

The first two Beatitudes relate to our proper relationship to self; the next two relate to our proper relationship to

God. Now notice the following three: the stage is set for a proper relationship to *others*. This is the progression of thought—Jesus' path to effective influence: to be effective in influencing others in a positive way, the four prerequisites must first be in place.

5. IF YOU HELP OTHERS

"Blessed are the merciful, for they shall receive mercy." (Matthew 5:7)

"Merciful" (*eleemon*, from which the English word *eleemosynary* is derived), refers to being beneficial or charitable. One who has *received* much *mercy* by way of the pardon of sin at the Cross, should display mercy, or charity, toward others.

> Those who are despondent over their sin, resulting in a whole-hearted pursuit of God, will show mercy to their fellow man.

Mercy carries the idea of *not* giving somebody what they deserve. God is merciful to the sinner in this way: He pardons the sinner. Accordingly, the beatitudinal believer displays mercy toward his fellow man. Such teachings by Jesus flies in the face of the smug Pharisees, who are void of mercy toward those who fail to measure up to their standards. Our influence on the Hill will be largely determined by our willingness to personally bless others, and our success in doing so.

Jesus states that the specific result of our mercifulness is that we will receive mercy. James 2:13 states this same promise in an opposite fashion: *"For judgment will be merciless to one who has shown no mercy"* (cf. Matthew 6:14–15). This is not to suggest that one gains salvation by being merciful; salvation is accomplished not by personal merit but by God's grace through trust in Christ. Rather, the idea is this: the degree to which we are merciful to others is the degree to which God is merciful to us. What goes around comes around. The idea is one of sowing and reaping; the one who sows mercy will reap mercy.

6. IF YOU ARE GENUINE WITH OTHERS

"Blessed are the pure in heart, for they shall see God." (Matthew 5:8)

When Jesus speaks these words in the Sermon on the Mount, Israel is in desperate straits. With a ripe history of disobedience to God, they find themselves under the control of an occupying foreign country, Rome, with an economy in shambles. They are under the religious misguidance of the leadership we discussed above. In that light, hearing Jesus say, "*Blessed are the pure in heart, for they shall see God,*" must have been liberating for those to whom he preached. The Pharisees in particular were not pure in heart—rather, falsely pious in heart—toward their fellow man. Theirs was a guilt-trip religion of never-ending proportions.

Given these insights and the contextual progression of the passage, Jesus is proclaiming in a positive way, "Don't be falsely pious toward your fellow man!" "Pure" (*katharos*) carries the sense of being cleansed from dirt and contamination. The Greek word is the basis of the English word *catharsis*, which refers to purging or evacuating. To be *pure in heart* means to be real in every way—especially emotionally! Don't coat your relationships with a thick layer of pharisaical super-spirituality as though you are perfect when everyone including yourself knows that you are not! Be authentic with others. It is the person who truthfully communicates transparency regarding personal brokenness over sin, but who is nonetheless passionate toward God and manifestly loving toward others, who is most attractive and influential in life. Genuine people become the greatest preservative and illuminative people in a nation. This is the kind of person others want to be around, not phony know-it-alls with plastic spirituality who act like they have it all together. Ugh!

The result of being pure in heart is intimacy with God: "*they shall see God.*" This phrase is in the future indicative tense and in the middle voice. It means, "they shall be continuously *seeing God* for themselves." In the progression of the Beatitudes we arrive at intimacy with God and others. What more could anyone desire?

7. IF YOU RECONCILE OTHERS TO GOD

> "*Blessed are the peacemakers, for they shall be called sons of God.*" (Matthew 5:9)

The third aspect of interpersonal relationship skills listed in the progression of the Beatitudes is that of being a messenger of peace to others. In that the believer has made peace with God, that person has become the ambassador of God's peace in the world. Every believer is an evangelist, sharing God's salvation with others—a *peacemaker* in the vertical sense. Again, note the progression: within the confines of horizontal relationships where one genuinely cares for others, we become able to effectively share Christ. Reconciling people to God in an eternal sense represents the ultimate in cultural preservation and illumination.

The Greek word used here for "sons" (*huios*) expresses the dignity and honor of a child to its parents. Synonymous with being an ambassador for Christ as depicted in 2 Corinthians 5:20 is the idea of being a *son of God*; both speak of being God's honorable representatives.

One would think the seven building blocks of virtue would result in great praise coming from others. Hardly. What results is just the opposite reaction from the world.

Two Reactive Effects: Matthew 5:10–11

The Biblical litmus test is this: one's experience of persecution and false accusation is proportional to how beatitudinal one is. If one is living an effective Christ-centered life characterized by these seven blessings, given the progression of this passage it is guaranteed that one will be persecuted and falsely accused. Expect nothing else, my friend. This will be the world's response, as well as the response of *tares* in the Church, to your godly living. If what follows is *not* your experience, then how spiritual are you really, according to Jesus' definition?

1. THEN YOU WILL BE PERSECUTED

> *"Blessed are those who have been persecuted for the sake of righteousness, for theirs is the kingdom of heaven."* (Matthew 5:10)

Second Timothy 3:12 stereophonically underscores this idea, "*All who desire to live godly in Christ Jesus will be persecuted.*"

Persecution is the evidence of true salvation and beatitudinal living. There will always be reaction, resentment, and jealously for those who live godly in Christ Jesus. Come to expect it—it is the believer's badge of authenticity. Don't be surprised!

2. THEN YOU WILL BE FALSELY ACCUSED

> *"Blessed are you when people insult you and persecute you, and falsely say all kinds of evil against you because of Me."* (Matthew 5:11)

Expect abusive words behind your back. If it was said of Jesus, "*Behold, a gluttonous man and a drunkard, a friend of tax collectors and sinners*" (Matthew 11:19), should you or I expect anything less? Being *falsely* accused for Christ's sake is a badge of authenticity.

One Rewarding Appropriation: Matthew 5:12

> *"Rejoice and be glad, for your reward in heaven is great; for in the same way they persecuted the prophets who were before you."* (Matthew 5:12)

Matthew 5:11–12 do not state that one who is persecuted and falsely accused for living beatitudinally should endure it with grief. No, it says one should feel blessed. This is worth underscoring! Note in the beginning of this passage the same idea: *"Rejoice and be glad, for your reward in heaven is great."* In times of persecution and false accusations align your emotional response with how God sees the matter. Don't be down! God views you as honorable. Commentator Pink states adroitly, "It is strong proof of human depravity that men's curses and Christ's blessings should meet on the same persons."[1] The believer is to "be glad" (*agalliao*), which is an imperative command meaning "to be overjoyed" in response to persecution. The King James Version of the Bible perhaps better captures this when it translates *"be glad"* as *"be exceeding glad."* Believers are commanded to respond not with doubt or sorrow over persecution, but rather they are to *skip and jump with happy excitement* that they are building eternal rewards.

Reacting maturely to others' negative responses to your godly living should be the norm in your life, as illustrated by *"the prophets who were before you."* What great company to keep!

Two Resulting Assessments: Matthew 5:13–14

1. PRESERVATION IN SOCIETY

> *"You are the salt of the earth; but if the salt has become tasteless, how can it be made salty again? It is no longer good for anything, except to be thrown out and trampled under foot by men."* (Matthew 5:13)

Salt is an appropriate metaphor in an ancient, non-refrigerated society. Salt was applied to meat in order to cure it and keep it from spoiling. In a similar sense, the believer who lives in a godly manner will influence others and society for good. Spirit-filled Christians retard moral and spiritual spoilage by their maturity in Christ. Their character, actions, and policies are for the betterment of all in this world.

What follows in this passage, *"but if the salt has become tasteless, how can it be made salty again,"* is a warning against the failure of the beatitudinal progression. Said another way, if you are not beatitudinal, in reality you are not a preserver of moral and spiritual godliness in society.

2. ILLUMINATION TO SOCIETY

"You are the light of the world. A city set on a hill cannot be hidden." (Matthew 5:14)

The second indicator of spiritual maturity and beatitudinal living is your luminous output. That is, how much *light* do you cast on your surroundings? While salt works to preserve behind the scenes, light openly illuminates. It *"cannot be hidden."* Indicative of a beatitudinal believer is his conspicuous presence! The believing Public Servant must be about proclaiming the excellences of Him who called him. States 1 Peter 2:9, *"But you are A CHOSEN RACE, A royal PRIESTHOOD, A HOLY NATION, A PEOPLE FOR God's OWN POSSESSION, so that you may proclaim the excellencies of Him who has called you out of darkness into His marvelous light."* Illumination of God's ways is normative behavior for Christ's ambassadors. Many more are needed in D.C.!

The influence of salt and light is an indication of beatitudinal maturity in the life of the believer. A news article that quoted Pew Research findings since the November 2016 elections shows that 91 percent of Congress describe themselves as Christians.[2] As a caution, we would be wise to consider Pew Research Center's qualifier here: "describe themselves as Christians." From the Pew information, it is impossible to determine whether these Congressmen consider Jesus Christ to be their personal Savior, which is the historic, traditional definition of a Christian, or consider Him to be merely a good example and not a Redeemer, as is preached by many liberal theologians today. Pew is not equipped to distinguish Christians from those who merely identify in that category without pursuing the faith. Yet even presuming the percentage of traditional Christians is much lower than 91 percent, the question remains:

Why aren't the committed Christians more effective in Congress?

Could it be that the believers on the Hill are not living out Jesus' Beatitudes? If they were we would see the preservation and illumination of America! Pray the Holy Spirit will impart beatitudinal characteristics in your life so you can maximize your influence on the hill. The degree to which you are beatitudinal is the degree to which you are influential.

Having recognized that the process of Christian maturing builds from one precept to another, hopefully it is clear to you that you can't get anywhere without a commitment to study of the Word of God. We'll look at that next.

Notes

1 Arthur W. Pink, "The Doctrine of Human Depravity: Its Evidences by Arthur W. Pink," *Grace Online Library*, accessed March 12, 2018, https://graceonlinelibrary.org/reformed-theology/total-depravity/the-doctrine-of-human-depravity-its-evidences-by-arthur-w-pink/.

2 "Faith on the Hill: The religious composition of the 115th Congress," accessed October 25, 2017, http://www.pewforum.org/2017/01/03/faith-on-the-hill-115/#fnref-27321-1.

"Go therefore and make disciples of all the nations … teaching them to observe all that I commanded you."

MATTHEW 28:19–20

"For I did not shrink from declaring to you the whole purpose of God."

ACTS 20:27

CHAPTER 4

Is Studying the Bible All That Important in Office?

In my years of ministry here in D.C., and before that in the California State Capitol building, I have often heard the following excuses surface regarding Bible study. Do any of these thoughts come to mind as you ponder the subject?

- "Some people worship the Bible rather than Jesus."

- "Right now in my life, fellowship is more important than studying the Bible."

- "Studying doctrine can be divisive, so I'd rather just love Jesus."

Each of these excuses is sometimes used as a "spiritual" reason why someone refrains from involvement in serious Bible study. Notice I didn't include "I just don't have the time." Elected leaders are too smart to suggest this excuse because both they and I know that time is a function of priorities, so to say that is to admit Bible study is not a priority.

Let's address each of these three excuses, as well as some practical benefits of a habitual lifetime of study. As a result you will gain a greater conviction to diligently study the Word of God and develop habits for a lifetime!

Before addressing each one of these excuses individually, let's start with what Jesus said in the Great Commission of Matthew 28:19–20 (the last words of instruction spoken by Him to His followers prior to His ascension into heaven):

> *"Go therefore and make disciples of all the nations … teaching them to observe all that I commanded you."*

We see the words *teaching them* combined with the word *all*. One of many implications of this passage is God's expectation that we will know *all* of His book. This point is further underscored by the apostle Paul in the book of Acts (Acts 20:27). Luke records Paul's interaction with the visiting Ephesian elders, where Paul says to them:

> *"For I did not shrink from declaring to you the whole purpose of God."*

From these two passages we get the powerful message that God expects His followers to know His Book—*all* and in *whole*! Beloved, it stands to reason that you cannot live by God's precepts if you don't know them in their entirety. On the other hand, if you choose to obey only a portion of them, you deem yourself, and not the Lord whom you claim to serve, to be the final authority!

Further, in the Great Commission passage God calls us to be His *disciples*. It is important to know exactly what the word *disciple* means. "Disciple" is the Greek word *mathetcuo*, which means "a learner." From there we see *math*, the root of the English word *mathematics*, "indicating thought accompanied by endeavor." Perhaps you can see where I am going with this: believers who are intent on spiritual growth must by definition be in a continual pursuit of Biblical learning, accompanied by endeavor.

I like to think of the Greek word *math* in terms of someone who can calculate: a disciple is someone who can calculate the world in which they live through the lens of Scripture. That is what it means to be a disciple, and lest you think you might have to go it alone, God has given you pastor-teachers to equip you in and with the Word of God in order for you to become wise at calculating all matters in life through Scripture. Ephesians 4:11 states this:

> *And He gave some … as evangelists, and some as pastors and teachers, for the equipping of the saints for the work of service, to the building up of the body of Christ.*

In Scripture *mathetes* is often juxtaposed to *didaskalos*, meaning "teacher."

A disciple then is defined as an endeavoring, calculating Biblical thinker who is sitting under at least one God-given pastor-teacher. In summary, it is Biblically incongruous to posture oneself as a maturing believer while failing in one's dedication to regular Bible study. Unfortunately today on the other side of the equation we see the vast majority of American churches serving up sermons devoid of much in the way of serious Bible study. Which is to say, I realize it is not easy to be a disciple, and it becomes impossible if you rationalize away serious Bible study using any one of the three excuses above. Now we're ready to look at these excuses more closely.

You Must Not Rationalize Away the Word of God

"SOME PEOPLE WORSHIP THE BIBLE RATHER THAN JESUS."

Notice the inseparability of God from His Word in the following two passages: Psalm 138:2 states:

> *I will worship toward thy holy temple, and praise thy name for thy lovingkindness and for thy truth: for thou hast magnified thy word above all thy name.* (KJV)

God and His Word are inseparable in this psalm. Additionally, Jesus is identified with the Word in the first chapter of John's Gospel, as seen in verses 1 and 14:

> *In the beginning was the Word, and the Word was with God, and the Word was God.*

> *And the Word became flesh, and dwelt among us, and we saw His glory, glory as of the only begotten from the Father, full of grace and truth.*

As if those two passages were not enough, Psalm 33:6 credits the Word of God with creation; God literally speaks the universe into existence:

> *By the word of the* Lord *the heavens were made, And by the breath of His mouth all their host.*

Colossians 1:16 also credits Jesus with creation:

> *For by Him all things were created, both in the heavens and on earth, visible and invisible, whether thrones or dominions or rulers or authorities—all things have been created through Him and for Him.*

Many similar passages could be cited, but suffice it to say that to separate Jesus from the Bible and the Bible from

Jesus is to build a false dichotomy relative to worship—a ludicrous and naïve position. To worship Jesus is to worship His Bible, and to worship His Bible is to worship Jesus. Second Timothy 3:16 cements the point:

> *All Scripture is inspired by God and profitable for teaching, for reproof, for correction, for training in righteousness.*

The Greek word for "Scripture" is *graphe* and the Greek word for "inspired" is *theopneustos*. The first word means "a writing" and the second means "inspired by God." In this passage, Paul is saying the written Word *is inspired by God*. Therefore, it just doesn't make sense to say one loves Jesus while ignoring the Bible. To disregard or discount the Word is to disregard or discount Jesus.

"RIGHT NOW IN MY LIFE, FELLOWSHIP IS MORE IMPORTANT THAN STUDYING THE BIBLE."

I have heard this statement bantered about in the Capital quite a lot over the years and I sometimes wonder who is propagating it. The convolution of the statement begs the question, what is true Christian fellowship? Philemon 1:6 states:

> *And I pray that the fellowship of your faith may become effective through the knowledge of every good thing which is in you for Christ's sake.*

Paul is instructing Philemon that true *fellowship* among believers is directly related to *knowledge* of one's identity in Christ, which knowledge can only be gained by diligent study of the Word of God. First John 1:7 states in this regard:

> *But if we walk in the Light as He Himself is in the Light, we have fellowship with one another.*

To the extent that we are illuminated by His Word we can achieve genuine fellowship with one another. Scripture is clear that true fellowship can only be achieved between true believers. Note 2 Corinthians 6:14:

> *What fellowship has light with darkness?*

It follows then that "Fellowship groups" devoid of authoritative Bible study accomplish little in terms of spiritual maturity in the lives of their members. They can be likened to folks who say they want to get in shape, but who go to the coffee house rather than the gym.

"STUDYING DOCTRINE CAN BE DIVISIVE, SO I'D RATHER JUST LOVE JESUS."

This statement is an oxymoron (a combination of contradictory or incongruous words).[1] Why? Because whenever one mentions the name of Jesus one is representing some kind of doctrine! Who exactly is the one you are mentioning and say you love? Is He God incarnate? Is He the LORD of the universe? Does He call people to repentance? Is Jesus the only way to God? Notice what Jesus Himself says about divisiveness in Matthew 10:34:

"Do not think that I came to bring peace on the earth; I did not come to bring peace, but a sword."

Later on in the same passage (v. 37) Jesus talks about how following Him may even cause division in one's earthly family:

"He who loves father or mother more than Me is not worthy of Me; and he who loves son or daughter more than Me is not worthy of Me."

For those who are intent on following Christ, the objective is to proclaim who He is, not to represent Him in such a way that you can garner the greatest personal acceptance. Therefore, to reason that believers should avoid Bible study because they may hear doctrine with which others might disagree is simply Biblically uninformed rationalization. The Jesus of the Bible did not come to teach us about some fuzzy, New Age, humanistic idea of "love." On the contrary:

> The Jesus of the Scriptures calls us to redemption through repentance from sin, and confronting sin inevitably creates divisions among people.

That doesn't mean we shouldn't be loving in our proclamation of Jesus, but we should be aware that in proclaiming Jesus others might become offended. As a matter of fact, Jesus says in Matthew 10:22:

"You will be hated by all because of My name, but it is the one who has endured to the end who will be saved."

Jesus calls people to make decisions about what they believe, which inevitably leads to divided opinions about Him.

These are just three of the many "spiritualized" excuses people come up with for avoiding serious Bible study. Rather than spend any more time examining how some people rationalize away the preeminence and authority of the Word of God, let's examine what God Himself says about the Word of God in the book of Proverbs. What did Solomon point out to a future political leader—his son, Rehoboam, to whom most of Proverbs is written—regarding the Word of God? I think you will find it quite fascinating!

You Must Regard Highly the Word of God

He who gives attention to the word will find good, and blessed is he who trusts in the LORD. (Proverbs 16:20)

In contrast to those who rationalize away the Word, notice Solomon's use of the term "gives attention" (*sakal*), meaning "to be prudent." We might understand this as meaning, "to concern oneself with or take notice of something: have regard or pay attention." The leader who highly regards "*the Word will find good.*" Many additional proverbs underscore and elaborate on this principle:

He who keeps the commandment keeps his soul, but he who is careless of conduct will die. (Proverbs 19:16)

One of the repetitive themes of Proverbs is the disciplined, prudent inner life. When you make a habit of *keeping* God's *commandments* and living in reverence towards Him, you will generally find a good life in this world. Often, if not always, those who lose their soul have a life-long history of aggressive or passive rebellion against the precepts of God.

It is important to note from this proverb (and all the others) that Solomon emphasizes to Rehoboam the need to give attention to and have regard for his inner life. Missing is any kind of parallel emphasis for him to stress governmental programs in his future state leadership. Such a priority should be true of you as well. This is how you keep from *dying*, so to speak, while holding office with all its various pressures.

You Must Rely Heavily on the Word of God

Every word of God is tested; He is a shield to those who take refuge in Him. (Proverbs 30:5)

Again, in stark contrast to the elected leader who rationalizes away the preeminence of the Word of God in his life, this passage is a tremendous confidence-builder for the Public Servants who choose to base their political ideology on the Word of God! Why? Because the Word of God is already "tested" (*tsaraph*), meaning "to smelt, refine." If you properly understand the Word, you can rely on it to inform you as to how to vote. The Word of God can refine and direct your thinking. This means you can argue from Scriptural positions in public debate, and later never find yourself in want for having taken the wrong position! God's tested Word can be a wonderful *shield* for your political ideology if you will rely on it! There is peace and *refuge* in holding to Biblical positions. Too often members of Congress who foolishly cast Biblically uninformed votes end up severely harming themselves and the country.

In a sense, God has already done much of your thinking for you. In support of the notion that leaders should hold to Biblically guided positions on policy matters, Psalms 119:2–4 and 46 express this powerfully and poignantly:

> *Blessed are those who observe His testimonies .... You have ordained your precepts .... I will also speak of Your testimonies before kings and shall not be ashamed.*

Therein is the confidence Solomon and David had in holding to the tested Word of God in their public lives as state leaders! As a result, they were never ashamed of a position they took. Today's lawmakers can rest their heads at night when their positions are steeped in the precepts of God's Holy Word. You can rely on the Word of God when you cast your vote, and not be ashamed.

You Must Be Restricted by the Word of God

> *Do not add to His words or He will reprove you, and you will be proved a liar.* (Proverbs 30:6)

It is important not to read into the Word of God, attempting to justify life decisions or policy positions that are not Biblically supported. That would be tantamount to *adding* to the Word of God. Where Scripture is dogmatic, one must be dogmatic, and where it is more of a compass than a road map, you should look to incorporate its principles to support policy positions. Reason from Scripture rather than reading into Scripture what you want it to say. Solomon echoes in this proverb a directive that recurs throughout the Bible: God's revelation is not an open matter. Scripture is no longer being written. Note Revelation 22:18–19 in support of this point and application:

> *I testify to everyone who hears the words of the prophecy of this book: if anyone adds to them, God will add to him the plagues which are written in this book; and if anyone takes away from the words of the book of this prophecy, God will take away his part from the tree of life and from the holy city, which are written in this book.*

The point of application is to refrain from playing loose with Scripture in support of policy when Scripture speaks to the contrary or does not speak specifically to an issue. Often, even when not explicit, Scripture will provide principles that may serve to support or deny a policy. And if that is the case, those principles should be cited. But do not attempt to make Scripture state something that it does not. When members toss in Scriptures grossly out of context while debating on the floor, I often think of the above passage from the book of Revelation. In essence, the presenter is *adding* to Scripture something that is not there. There should be—and there are—restrictions to one's use of the Word. Don't be flippant with it, lest God *reprove you* for mishandling His book.

The Results of Obedience to the Word of God

> *The one who despises the word will be in debt to it, But the one who fears the commandment will be rewarded.* (Proverbs 13:13)

God *rewards* those who are students of His book! In this proverb Solomon is instructing every state leader with two contrasting truths: destruction awaits one who *despises* God's revelation, while rewarding one who *fears* the Bible. There are rewards from God inuring to the benefit of the one who studies and obeys God's Word. Garrett aptly comments on the meaning of this proverb:

> Every person desires to see his or her longings fulfilled. In the wisdom of the world, the way to success is through diligent effort. There is truth in this…. Yet the Bible goes beyond the secular wisdom of relating success to hard work and more fundamentally ties it to the development of a mature, virtuous soul by submission to wise teachers. Diligence is thus the fruit of a soul that has cultivated goodness, and success follows naturally.[2]

This is a wonderful summary of Proverbs' formula for success. The psalmist echoes these sentiments when he pens Psalms 119:11 and 97:

> *Your word I have treasured in my heart, that I may not sin against You…. O how I love Your law! It is my meditation all the day.*

Surely there is reward for those who make the regular intake of the Word a priority, leading to study under solid, motivational Bible teachers whom God has given to His people. God has placed them in the world to help you meditate on His Word. So, utilize them!

Athletes do not reach their potential apart from coaches,
nor do believers apart from Bible teachers.

Much can be gained from Solomon's insights on this subject. In these passages from Proverbs, the wisest human who ever lived is attempting to pass along his own awed and humble view of Scripture to his son who would become king. Given this close parallel to your life, don't rationalize or spiritualize away the preeminence that Scripture must have continually in and throughout your life.

The Bible Is Revelation from God

The repeated testimony of the Bible is that it is the written revelation from God to mankind. This is the clear testimony of its writers. In 2 Timothy 3:16–17, 1 Thessalonians 2:13 and 2 Peter 1:20–21, we read from the pens of apostles Paul and Peter respectively:

All Scripture is inspired by God and profitable for teaching, for reproof, for correction, for training in righteousness; so that the man of God may be adequate, equipped for every good work.

For this reason we also constantly thank God that when you received the word of God which you heard from us, you accepted it not as the word of men, but for what it really is, the word of God, which also performs its work in you who believe.

But know this first of all, that no prophecy of Scripture is a matter of one's own interpretation, for no prophecy was ever made by an act of human will, but men moved by the Holy Spirit spoke from God.

Thousands of other passages attest to the godly origin of the Bible. As simple as is the truth that the Bible is revelation from God, it is easy to overlook the profundity of what that should mean in terms of our response and allegiance to it. What follows are some of the many benefits of becoming a disciplined student of His Book.

THE FIFTEEN BENEFITS

What are some of the practical benefits of a habitual lifetime of study? I can think of fifteen benefits that God Himself speaks of about this matter. What follows should motivate you to increase your personal Bible study habit! I will briefly touch on each with the hope that you will gain an overall compelling picture (some points you'll notice tend to overlap a bit) pertaining to your own study habits. My hope is that you will gain a greater desire to diligently absorb the Word of God on a regular basis.

1. The Word of God will assure you of your salvation

So faith comes from hearing, and hearing by the word of Christ. (Romans 10:17)

Saving *faith* comes from *hearing* the message about Christ; the unadulterated Gospel message is codified in the Scriptures. Without the *Word of Christ*, how would we know that we are saved through faith in Christ alone? We would be lost in various opinions.

2. The Word of God will teach you

All Scripture is inspired by God and profitable for teaching, for reproof, for correction, for training in righteousness; so that the man of God may be adequate, equipped for every good work. (2 Timothy 3:16–17)

It is the Bible that contains the total truth necessary for living a life that is pleasing to one's Maker in every way! It is the basis for one's confidence in the standards of right and wrong. There are other sources of truth in the world, but their certainty is less than that of *all Scripture*. You can be certain that what you are doing is right when it is based on God's Word.

3. The Word of God will guide you

For the commandment is a lamp and the teaching is light; And reproofs for discipline are the way of life. (Proverbs 6:23)

Your word is a lamp to my feet And a light to my path. (Psalm 119:105)

The words *commandment*, *teaching*, *discipline*, *lamp*, and *light* all represent God's Word. Like a flashlight on a dark night, it will keep you from stumbling down the path of life. You can walk with surety when what the Bible has taught you guides you every step of the way!

4. The Word of God will counsel you

Your commandments make me wiser than my enemies, For they are ever mine. (Psalm 119:98)

Your testimonies also are my delight; They are my counselors. (Psalm 119:24)

You can be consistently correct not only in the decisions you make in your personal life, but on the positions you take on government policies. I once heard a presidential candidate say that he thought religion was good for his personal life, but that it did not necessarily inform his policy decisions. How sad, I thought to myself. Learn and hold on to God's principles! They are unfailing, unchanging, and always correct for every area of your life. Remember that you live to please only one person: your Maker who has revealed Himself to you in His Word, whom you will face in the day of judgment. Allow Him to counsel you every day you live!

5. The Word of God will restore you

The law of the LORD is perfect, restoring the soul; The testimony of the LORD is sure, making wise the simple. (Psalm 19:7)

This passage means that the teachings of the LORD will turn back your *soul*. Said another way, God's Word has the power to revive the inner man and strengthen you in times of despondency. It will make you *wise* and help you learn from mistakes so you will not repeat them over and over again.

6. The Word of God will warn you

Moreover, by them Your servant is warned; In keeping them there is great reward. (Psalm 19:11)

The pronoun *them* refers to the Scriptures. Most of the problems we face in life are self-induced, directly related to our ignorance of or willful disobedience to Scriptural principles. To know Scripture intimately is to inform and bolster your conscience so that in times of temptation you will be strong enough to do what is Biblically correct. If you prioritize the time and discipline to place Scripture in your mind, the Holy Spirit will be faithful to use it to *warn* of danger—to convict. You will be spiritually stronger to avoid sin if you have a consistent habit of Bible study (the opposite is also true). As we read earlier in Proverbs 13:13, "*The one who despises the word will be in debt to it, But the one who fears the commandment will be rewarded.*" There is *great reward* in *keeping* to Scripture.

7. The Word of God will nourish you

Like newborn babies, long for the pure milk of the word, so that by it you may grow in respect to salvation. (1 Peter 2:2)

Revealed in this passage is the formula for growth:

There is no consistent growth without a consistent intake of Biblical nourishment.

Do you *"long for the pure milk of the Word"*? That is the formula for growth. This truth is why Biblical feeding is the primary responsibility of a good shepherd toward his sheep. In this regard the apostle Paul instructs all future pastors to center in on the following:

> *In pointing out these things to the brethren, you will be a good servant of Christ Jesus, constantly nourished on the words of the faith and of the sound doctrine which you have been following.* (1 Timothy 4:6)

Watch out for ministers who are not *constantly nourished* and are therefore unable to feed others with the Word. Prioritize being around ministers and ministries that feed you God's Word consistently.

8. The Word of God will judge you

> *For the word of God is living and active and sharper than any two-edged sword, and piercing as far as the division of soul and spirit, of both joints and marrow, and able to judge the thoughts and intentions of the heart.* (Hebrews 4:12)

This passage is loaded with profundities! Suffice it to say that God's Word exposes false believers and disobedient believers. It is *living and active*! This truth is underscored by:

> *So will My word be which goes forth from My mouth; It will not return to Me empty, Without accomplishing what I desire, And without succeeding in the matter for which I sent it.* (Isaiah 55:11)

When the Word is proclaimed it never *returns empty*. In its proclamation, it always *accomplishes* what God *desires*. Often times it serves to expose the real motives and intentions of men's hearts. For the sensitive believer, such exposure is welcome because it leads to repentance and growth.

9. The Word of God will sanctify you

> *Sanctify them in the truth; Your word is truth.* (John 17:17)

The word *sanctify* as it is used throughout Scripture means set apart for Christian maturation. One grows through grappling with the *truth*, and ultimate truth is only found in the Scriptures. This fact is stated again as Christ's intended way of maturing His Church:

> *That He might sanctify her, having cleansed her by the washing of water with the word.* (Ephesians 5:26)

10. The Word of God will free you

> *So Jesus was saying to those Jews who had believed Him, "If you continue in My word, then you are truly disciples of Mine; and you will know the truth, and the truth will make you free."* (John 8:31–32)

True believers always hunger to be obedient to the Word. As stated earlier, the Greek root for "disciples" (*mathetes*) means more than "followers." The Greek root is the same word from which we derive the word "math," meaning you will have the ability to calculate the will of God in a matter. *True disciples* always want to know more about God and want to be obedient to Him and discern—make a calculation—regarding His way in their lives. Conversely, if they have no desire for learning the Word and being obedient to God, then they are fooling themselves into thinking they are saved when the Biblical evidence clearly indicates otherwise (cf. 2 John 1:9). What results? The truly redeemed have a deep-seated sense of sheer *freedom* from the weight and inevitable consequences of sin.

11. The Word of God will enrich you

> *Let the word of Christ richly dwell within you, with all wisdom teaching and admonishing one another with psalms and hymns and spiritual songs, singing with thankfulness in your hearts to God.* (Colossians 3:16)

Richly dwell means to dwell "extravagantly" or "abundantly." The *Word of Christ* refers to the whole of Scripture. As God's Word saturates and controls your life, you will live *enriched* and overflowing with *thankfulness* to God—positively pouring over into others' lives!

12. The Word of God will protect you

> *Your word I have treasured in my heart, That I may not sin against You.* (Psalm 119:11)

How does one live with less *sin*? The key to overcoming sin is to *treasure* God's *Word* in one's *heart*. The Evangelist Dwight L. Moody said, "The Bible will keep you from sin, or sin will keep you from the Bible."[3]

13. The Word of God will strengthen you

> *My soul weeps because of grief; Strengthen me according to Your word.* (Psalm 119:28)

The result of sin is agony, guilt, loss of vigor, and broken relationships (to mention a few). The psalmist's remedy? Be *strengthened* by the *Word*.

14. The Word of God will embolden you

> *Even though princes sit and talk against me, Your servant meditates on Your statutes.* (Psalm 119:23)

Do you want to have the courage to unashamedly do what is right no matter what the pressure is from others? *Meditate* on the Word! Set your mind to please God, versus paying attention to others whose plans may run contrary to God's testimonies.

15. The Word of God will stabilize you

> *He will be like a tree firmly planted by streams of water, Which yields its fruit in its season And its leaf does not wither; And in whatever he does, he prospers.* (Psalm 1:3)

Over the years, I have seen many "Christian" Legislators *wither*. They come and go because they violate this principle of meditating on the Word. Unfortunately, "*they are like chaff which the wind drives away*" (Psalm 1:4). God doesn't honor them and suddenly they are out. It saddens my heart to so often see this. They are "*double-minded … unstable in all [their] ways*" (James 1:8). Conversely:

> "*This book of the law shall not depart from your mouth, but you shall meditate on it day and night, so that you may be careful to do according to all that is written in it; for then you will make your way prosperous, and then you will have success. Have I not commanded you? Be strong and courageous! Do not tremble or be dismayed, for the* LORD *your God is with you wherever you go.*" (Joshua 1:8–9)

These passages promise *prosperity* and *success* to those who *meditate* on the Word *day and night*!

By now you see why you must not rationalize away, but rather emphasize the study of Scripture every day, and why you need to be serious about habitual study over a lifetime! Consistent, prioritized Bible study is what you really need if you are to remain strong on the Hill. This is how you will begin to see the transformative work of sanctification take place in your life. Are you inspired to make fresh commitments in this regard today?

Notes

1 By permission. From Merriam-Webster.com © 2017 by Merriam-Webster, Inc. https://www.merriam-webster.com/dictionary/oxymoron.

2 Duane A. Garrett, *The New American Commentary*, Vol. 14 (Nashville: B&H Publishing Group, 1993), 138.

3 "Dwight L. Moody Quotes," *Good Reads*, accessed March 12, 2018, https://www.goodreads.com/author/quotes/5083573.D_L_Moody.

... that, in reference to your former manner of life, you lay aside the old self, which is being corrupted in accordance with the lusts of deceit, and that you be renewed in the spirit of your mind, and put on the new self, which in the likeness of God has been created in righteousness and holiness of the truth.

EPHESIANS 4:22–24

CHAPTER 5

How to Effect Change and Growth in Your Life

Sanctification is God's process of spiritual growth that the believer should experience throughout his entire life. It is a progressive work and its purpose is to enable the believer to resist his own carnal human urges, die to sin, and live in righteousness. Through the sanctification process, the believer makes decisions that enable him to become more Christlike. Sanctification frees the believer from destructive behaviors that separate him from God; sinful habits are systematically mortified.

Sanctification is the process of transformation, of spiritual maturation. As we will see from the exegesis that follows, it is a continuous work of God's grace, meaning to make holy, purify, to be set apart for holy use. What specifically does God's Word identify as the key ingredient that enables God's sanctifying process? Additionally, what are some of the misguided man-made, get-closer-to-God theories that we should avoid?

The Bible has much to say about how a person can change; as a matter of fact, the Scriptures reveal that those who are in Christ *will* change for the better.[1] But how exactly does this happen? Or better, how is the believer sanctified, to use the appropriate theological term? There are at least four major historical/theological views proffered in answer to this, but as you will see, only one of them has a solid Biblical basis. Very briefly they are:

1. TOTAL PERFECTIONISM

The first is known as *Christian Perfectionism*. It stems from Charles Wesley, the historic English leader of the Methodist movement. Herein a supposed second post-salvation work of grace catapults the believer into a state of "sinlessness." Another name for this flawed view is *Entire Sanctification*. The believer may make mistakes, but supposedly he is no longer sinning. Spiritual growth is indicated by increasing good works. Simply put in a real-world sense, Wesleyan Perfectionism is problematic in that one only need ask the perfect person's spouse if he or she is perfect. Practical reality suggests that total sanctification/perfection is not achieved by any believer in this life. Nor is such a view supported by Scripture.

> *For it is God who is at work in you, both to will and to work for His good pleasure.* (Philippians 2:13)

2. PASSIVE GROWTH

A second widely held view of sanctification is the *Keswick* (pronounced "Kezeek") school of thinking. In this understanding believers passively grow in their relationship to Christ. One need only "surrender" to grow spiritually. Just keep drinking in the Bible and you will mature. "Let go and let God" is an appropriate summary of this way of thinking. But as will be seen in what follows, God's grace enables human responsibility in the sanctification process and there is a Biblical expectation of human volition in the achievement of spiritual growth.

3. PENANCE AND REMORSE

This third position is commonly practiced in cults. It is known as *penance*. Whereas the previous two positions are practiced in error amongst those with a Biblical soteriology (that is, a proper understanding of what the Bible teaches about true saving faith), penance is the idea of imposing a punishment for sin in a human attempt to balance the scales. In the world of penance-seekers, neither justification (one's salvation) nor sanctification (one's spiritual growth) is imputed from God via His enablement (as per the truths of 1 John 1:9 and many other passages). Rather, one's salvation and sanctification are earned by way of self-effort or personal merit. In this way of thinking it follows that if one is saved by personal merit, one also grows by personal merit. One is sanctified by practicing good deeds or prayers in order to propitiate (satisfy) one's wrongdoings; one is "guilted" into changing. The problem is, like the former positions, there is no Biblical basis for such a belief or practice.

4. PROGRESSIVE SANCTIFICATION

The fourth position on sanctification is the one that is supported by Scripture: *Progressive Sanctification*. The Bible repeatedly reveals that a lifelong cycle of repentance and renewal progresses us toward Christlikeness, and this process of growth will only be complete when we go home to be with the Lord. There is no perfection this side of heaven. Growth and change are accomplished through the active participation and discipline of the believer, whom the Holy Spirit prompts and energizes for the task. Philippians 2:12–13 and many other passages support this summation on sanctification:

> *So then, my beloved, just as you have always obeyed, not as in my presence only, but now much more in my absence, work out your salvation with fear and trembling; for it is God who is at work in you, both to will and to work for His good pleasure.*

Notice this passage closely. "Work out" (the Greek word *katergazomai*) is not referring to salvation by works[2] (cf. Romans 3:21–24; Ephesians 2:8, 9; John 1:12; Romans 10:9), but rather is descriptive of the responsibility that believers must possess after being saved by God's grace. And the words *"it is God who is at work in you"* evidence the causal agent (God), who engenders and empowers the *working out* of sanctification in the lives of believers after being saved. Other passages that support the Biblical teaching of Progressive Sanctification are Philippians 3:13–14; Romans 6:19; Acts 1:8; 1 Corinthians 9:24–27; 15:58; 2 Corinthians 7:1; Galatians 6:7–9; Ephesians 4:1; Colossians 3:1–17; Hebrews 6:10–11; 12:1–2; and 2 Peter 1:5–11. Each passage underscores Progressive Sanctification, wherein *"God who is at work in you"* is the One who prompts believers, and the believers have a responsibility to work—to achieve spiritual growth as God directs in their hearts.

Scriptural Basics Related to Sanctification

The aforementioned list of Bible passages is worth pondering. In summary all these Scriptures speak of human responsibility—that is, working at your sanctification—as catalytic to change. But more specifically, how are we to work? What follows are the four Scriptural basics related to sanctification.

1. ALL CHANGES SHOULD ALIGN WITH SCRIPTURE

Since the Bible is inspired by God, it is the basis of all truth. "He is there and He is not silent,"[3] wrote Francis Schaeffer. In other words, God has revealed Himself to man not only in the advent of His Son Jesus Christ, but in His Holy Word. Scripture therefore must be the sole epistemological source (that is, the sole grounds for knowledge) as it relates to one's faith, practice, and changes. Notice Scripture's internal testimony regarding itself as it relates to change:

> *All Scripture is inspired by God and profitable for teaching, for reproof, for correction, for training in righteousness.*
> (2 Timothy 3:16)

The Greek construct of this important passage is best translated, "All Scripture is given by inspiration." Notice that one of the specific purposes for which God *inspired* Scripture is for proper *teaching*, *reproof*, *correction*, and *training*; all these words connote change that is informed and guided by Scriptural truths. Add to this understanding the following:

> *For this reason we also constantly thank God that when you received the word of God which you heard from us, you accepted it not as the word of men, but for what it really is, the word of God, which also performs its work in you who believe.* (1 Thessalonians 2:13)

Scripture states of itself that it intends to *perform a work in you*, that is, to change those who believe in it. Accordingly, since the Bible is God's Word to man, every change one desires to make should align with His ordinances.

The Scriptures are the basis for achieving right changes. Second Corinthians 10:5 echoes this very point when it says, "*taking every thought captive to the obedience of Christ.*"

2. ONE ADMONISHES ANOTHER WITH SCRIPTURE IN ORDER TO PRODUCE CHANGE

The second Scriptural basic related to change can be gleaned from 1 Thessalonians 5:14. Paul states, "*We urge you, brethren, admonish [noutheteo] the unruly, encourage the fainthearted, help the weak, be patient with everyone.*" Change occurs when one is confronted by the truths of God. Change results, according to 1 Corinthians 1:18, because God's

Word has power—power to change individuals when they are confronted by it:

> *For the word of the cross is foolishness to those who are perishing, but to us who are being saved it is the power of God.*

Isaiah 55:11 amplifies this same astounding truth:

> *So will My word be which goes forth from My mouth; It will not return to Me empty, Without accomplishing what I desire, And without succeeding in the matter for which I sent it.*

The Word of God is the conduit that one must utilize in counseling or mentoring (or better, *admonishing*) another to change. (Note that this is where the term *Nouthetic Counseling* comes from. This is a form of pastoral counseling that is totally Bible-based and focused solely on Christ. It renounces conventional psychology and psychiatry as humanistic because so often they are opposed to Biblical principles.) Hebrews 4:12 summarizes the importance of the Word to create change: "*For the word of God is living and active and sharper than any two-edged sword.*" Often God uses other believers through their spoken words or writings to amplify His Word in our lives. Look for this and be open to it. This is how God intends to create Biblically based change in your life.

3. THE REACTION TO SCRIPTURAL ADMONITION MUST BE REPENTANCE

Building from the first two Scriptural basics related to change is how you respond to being admonished by the Word of God. Pivotal to this understanding is 2 Timothy 2:25:

> *... with gentleness correcting those who are in opposition, if perhaps God may grant them repentance leading to the knowledge of the truth.*

The proper Biblical response to the admonitions of the Word of God is *not*, "I don't need to change; I am already perfect." Nor is it, "I'll just let go and let God." Nor is it, "I'll balance the scales myself." On the contrary, this passage reveals that "repentance" (*metanoia*), "to change one's mind or purpose," is the key to the believer's growth process. Scripture reveals here and elsewhere (cf. Acts 5:31; 11:18; Romans 2:4; 2 Corinthians 7:9–10; Ephesians 2:7; 2 Timothy 2:25) that *repentance* is produced by God's sovereign grace: "*if perhaps God may grant ...*"

In other words, like the faith to believe in Christ (Ephesians 2:8–9), repentance too is a gift from God! One who is trapped in sin and desires to change should therefore cry out in humility, "God have mercy on me and grant me the gift of repentance from my sin!"

Repentance leads to lasting change; it is the key element in Progressive Sanctification! Jeremiah 13:23 underscores this, saying that any change apart from God-given repentance is futile:

> *"Can the Ethiopian change his skin Or the leopard his spots? Then you also can do good Who are accustomed to doing evil."*

The point is that sinners in and of themselves cannot *change* the essence of their very nature. Therefore, the only way they can achieve lasting change is with God's help, which is why crying out to Him in brokenness and contrition is the only way one can initiate change for the better.

4. THE RECURRING PAULINE SOUND BITE DESCRIBING CHANGE

In Paul's letters to the Roman, Ephesian, and Colossian churches he often speaks of spiritual growth in terms of "putting off" and "putting on." He is saying that to grow spiritually, the believer must put off the old self and put on the new self. Ephesians 4:22–24 best encapsulates this:

> *… that, in reference to your former manner of life, you lay aside the old self, which is being corrupted in accordance with the lusts of deceit, and that you be renewed in the spirit of your mind, and put on the new self, which in the likeness of God has been created in righteousness and holiness of the truth.*

Key to our study of how believers effectuate change in their lives is the idea of *laying aside the old self*, or *putting it off*. The Greek word for "repentance," (*metanoia*), is synonymous with putting off or laying aside. It means to turn 180 degrees, to put off and out of your life what is not pleasing to God. It follows then that repentance, or putting off, is an essential element for Christian growth.

Given these four basics related to sanctification, how can we best understand characteristics of true repentance? What follows may seem a bit "in the weeds" on this subject, but precisely and thoroughly understanding what the Bible means by repentance is of utmost importance, since it is the starting point of spiritual growth! Conversely, to fail at this point is to fail at growing spiritually.

How do we recognize repentance according to the Bible? What is the difference between human sorrow and true repentance? Second Corinthians 7:9–11 is the passage in the New Testament that best delineates the characteristics of genuine repentance. Let us now turn our attention to how best to understand this passage.

The Context of the Instruction on True Repentance

I now rejoice, not that you were made sorrowful, but that you were made sorrowful to the point of repentance; for you were made sorrowful according to the will of God, so that you might not suffer loss in anything through us. For the sorrow that is according to the will of God produces a repentance without regret, leading to salvation, but the sorrow of the world produces death. For behold what earnestness this very thing, this godly sorrow, has produced in you: what vindication of yourselves, what indignation, what fear, what longing, what zeal, what avenging of wrong! In everything you demonstrated yourselves to be innocent in the matter. (2 Corinthians 7:9–11)

In this portion of 2 Corinthians Paul is tracing over the past relationship he has had with the Body of Believers in Corinth. In brief summary, during his second missionary journey he spends eighteen months personally establishing this church. Some time after planting this church he sends his emissary, Timothy, to Corinth (1 Corinthians 4:17; 16:10, 11). As a result Paul finds out that self-styled false apostles now inhabit the assembly, and in their zeal for power, they have castigated Paul and tried to persuade the congregation no longer to follow his teachings. When he learns this mutinous news, Paul immediately departs from Ephesus to visit Corinth. To his deep chagrin, upon his arrival he soon tastes of the bitter fruit of the false teachers, experiencing the disloyalty of many in the flock—a flock he labored so hard to establish. In response, upon his return to Ephesus he authors what is now commonly referred to as the *Severe Letter* (2 Corinthians 2:4), sending it to Corinth with his beloved, loyal disciple, Titus.

Upon Titus' eventual reconnection with Paul, Titus gives a surprisingly warm report to Paul about the Corinthian church's acceptance of Paul's Severe Letter. Specifically, many have *repented* of their rebellion against the apostle! Paul is overjoyed to learn of this, as we read above. It is in this context that the words of 2 Corinthians chapter 7 must be understood: as a result of the mutiny and the congregation's subsequent repentance, the Holy Spirit is revealing through this Scripture what characterizes true repentance in the life of the believer. Again, there is perhaps no better passage in the entire Bible to unveil poignant insights that all followers of Christ must possess for true repentance.

Eight Aspects of Genuine Repentance

True, genuine repentance, states Paul, is characterized by at least eight attitudes and related actions that grow from God's sanctifying presence in the life of the believer.[4] "Paul expands [on the *matter* of godly *sorrow*] into a whole series of acts or dispositions, all of which are inspired by that sorrow, according to God."[5] This list of eight follows from Paul's words in the passage:

1. EARNESTNESS (*SPOUDE*)

When believers experience godly *sorrow* they manifest a sense of *earnestness* to eagerly and assertively pursue a righteous course. There will be, as one commentator puts it, "speed involved in the carrying out of a matter,... a willingness to do good will."[6] This is the initial reaction of genuine repentance that is borne from above: the first earmark is that godly sorrow will produce *earnestness* of motivation. There is a resolution that becomes a reality, an internal motivation, an earnest desire to "*bear fruit in keeping with repentance*" (Matthew 3:8).

2. VINDICATION (*APOLOGIA*)

The New International Commentary on the New Testament (NICNT) states in regard to *vindication*, "When they [the unrepentant Corinthian believers] thought of the infamy which sin had brought upon the church, they were quite eager to clear themselves of complicity in it and angry with themselves that they had ever allowed such a thing to be."[7] Here is the second mark of true repentance, as one commentator puts it: "A desire to clear one's name of the stigma that accompanies sin. The repentant sinner restores the trust and confidence of others by making his genuine repentance known."[8] There comes an earnest desire to outwardly rectify, to *vindicate* that which the sin caused. Conversely, the falsely repentant are characterized by an attitude that remains stayed on self—far more concerned about damage to personal image than promptness to remedy. The unrepentant remain hung-up on themselves, and the ramifications to *self* that stem from their actions: their reputations and their standing amongst peers remain more important. True repentance is always accompanied by a God-given desire to immediately vindicate a matter, seeking out others that have been offended, asking for their forgiveness, and thereby redressing the wrong done. Put another way, to the genuinely repentant, outward self-preservation is less important than God-glorification. Where an unction to vindicate is missing, a person is really not repentant.

3. INDIGNATION (*AGANAKTESIS*)

The Greek word translated here into English as *indignation* is used elsewhere in several other Gospel narratives and carries the idea of being angered by one's own wrongful actions. The early church father Chrysostom interpreted this portion of the passage to mean that the authentically repentant believer will be characterized by a personal *indignation* or anger resulting from the affront against the church and against the name of God that he has allowed to occur. Here is another clear indication of genuine repentance: believers possess an internal hatred and anger over their sin and a discontent because of the *indignity* it has brought on the Lord's name and His Church. In actuality, this self-indignation is a blessing from God that can be likened to the internal molten pressure found in a volcano. There will be an authentic self-hatred that brews inside the believer's heart that can only find its release through total rectification with offended parties.

4. FEAR (*PHOBOS*)

In addition to their internal compunction, the wayward Corinthian believers *fear* the apostolic authority of the one to whom they had been disloyal. They fear that he could seek retribution for their sinful ways, in fact, "*with a rod*" (1 Corinthians 4:21). A manifest characteristic of true repentance is a healthy fear not only of God, but of those the sin has wronged.

To summarize the first four points:

**The genuinely repentant possess an earnest desire
to vindicate a wrong they have done, motivated by self-indignation
from a holy fear of God's and man's judgment.**

5. LONGING (*EPIPOTHESIS*)

Akin to *vindication*, which has in mind the outward demonstration of godly sorrow, *longing* relates more to a vehement inner desire stemming from the heart.[9] In their genuine repentance the Corinthian believers are impassioned by an internal longing to honor Paul and his apostolic authority. In addition, they strongly desire to repudiate the false intruders in the church. More deeply, they possess a yearning to follow Paul's example of wholehearted devotion to the cause of Christ.

All of these attitudes express a motivated-by-God compunction to do the right thing. Why? John Murray states, "[True] regeneration is the renewing of the heart and mind, and the renewed heart and mind must act according to their nature."[10] The genuinely repentant will always yearn for right relationships with others. In Romans 12:18 Paul embodies this when he states, "*If possible, so far as it depends on you, be at peace with all men.*"

6. ZEAL (*ZELOS*)

Another attitude that is consistent with true repentance is the *zeal* that the Corinthian believers possess to take up Paul's defense and stand against the false teachers who have taken over the Corinthian church. *Zelos* is the Greek word from which we derive the English word "jealousy." States NICNT, the Corinthian believers desired "to see the restoration of their former relationship of trust and affection."[11] Their response to Paul's Severe Letter is not one of anger, but one of sober realization that they have been disloyal to the apostle. They adopt Paul's view toward the false teachers and take up Paul's cause as their own! God-enabled genuine repentance produces this kind of zeal to do an about-face on a matter. They have zeal to reaffirm their love for and allegiance to him. On the other hand, people who are unrepentant or humanly sorrowful in a selfish way will remain disloyal to the cause of Christian restoration, and avoid self-examination regarding an offense. They are characterized by not admitting any wrongdoing, and blaming the other party.

7. AVENGING OF WRONG (*EKDIKESIS*)

Perhaps the strongest indication of true repentance is the one that is hardest to perform by means other than God-given. In God-empowered repentance, sinners overcome the impulse to protect themselves first; the overriding concern is for justice to be done. One commentator states, "he wants to see the sin avenged no matter what it might cost him."[12] It does not matter here whether Paul is referring in our home passage to the Corinthians *avenging wrong* in their interpersonal relationships, or in having allowed the false apostles to lead in the church. In both cases, the now-humbled Corinthian believers have a desire to seek reconciliation! The all-consuming objective is to put their house in order no matter the cost. When this is one's attitude, spiritual growth is in view:

<blockquote>

Progressive Sanctification occurs where there is an earnest desire to avenge the wrong that has been done.

</blockquote>

8. INNOCENT IN THE MATTER (*HAGNOS*)

The last aspect of genuine repentance that Paul chooses to express is *innocence*. The Greek word here for *innocent* means "clean," "pure," or "holy." He chooses this word because it has to do with ritual purity. Without going into greater details of early word use, the idea carried here is that if a procedure is followed, then purity results. And that is exactly why Paul places this word last on his list. Paul's word choice displays a beautiful, human illustration of the theology behind 1 John 1:9, which states:

If we confess our sins, He is faithful and righteous to forgive us of our sins and to cleanse us from all unrighteousness.

The Corinthian believers in Paul's mind are now innocent of the matter because they have *confessed* and repented of their *sin*, as is more than evident by the seven new attitudes and actions that precede this. It is also important to note that Paul doesn't rehash the sin here; he simply calls it *the matter*. Why? In that they have satisfactorily taken care of their sin, in Paul's mind the past has been made "*as white as snow*" (Isaiah 1:18) because they have borne "*fruit in keeping with repentance*" (Matthew 3:8). In Philippians we learn that Paul practices "*forgetting what lies behind*" (Philippians 3:13). Since the past has been made right, it is time to move on, not relive the sin. Paul is expressing an attitude of exhilaration over the completion of the matter. This passage then is a beautiful narrative of spiritual growth: dehabituation and rehabituation have been achieved.

These eight characteristics of genuine repentance are basic to spiritual growth: correctly and completely turning away from the past and moving toward what is right in the future; putting off and putting on; dehabituation and rehabituation.

A worldly kind of self-centered sorrow over sin will manifest few if any of these attitudes characteristic of true, genuine repentance. Furthermore, holding on to sin is stagnating to one's spiritual growth. Remember the Greek word for *repentance* means, "change of mind," whereas *lupe*, the Greek word for *worldly sorrow* means "pain of body." Repentance is the fundamental key to a life of change and growth. As such, we mature in our Christian life through genuine repentance. So then, as God places things on your heart that need to change, pay close attention! Turn from them in earnestness and put them behind you forever as you put off and put on, and move on toward sanctification in Christ! Amen!

As God sanctifies you, His *love* for humanity, as expressed through you, will begin to take on new importance. We will look at that next.

Notes

1 2 Corinthians 5:17 states, "Therefore if anyone is in Christ, he is a new creature; the old things passed away; behold, new things have come."

2 Salvation is explicitly revealed in Scripture to be a gift to those who will by faith repent and receive Jesus Christ as Lord.

3 Francis A. Schaeffer, *He Is There and He Is Not Silent* (Carol Stream, IL: Tyndale House, 1973).

4 As stated, repentance is actually a gift from God, given along with the ability to believe in Christ, at the day of one's salvation. Importantly and additionally, this gift of repentance is ongoing in its operation—not only in salvation, but in sanctification (throughout the life of the believer), as implied by the apostle in this passage under study.

5 "Bible Commentaries, Expositor's Bible Commentary, 2 Corinthians 7," *Study Light*, accessed March 15, 2018, https://www.studylight.org/commentaries/teb/2-corinthians-7.html.

6 Colin Brown, ed., *New International Dictionary of New Testament Theology* (Grand Rapids: Zondervan, 1986).

7 Philip Edgcumbe Hughes, *The New International Commentary on the New Testament: Paul's Second Epistle to the Corinthians* (Grand Rapids: Eerdmans, 1962).

8 Landon Chapman, "Is It Enough to Just Be Sorry?: An Exposition of Biblical Repentance," June 13, 2014, *Entreating Favor*, accessed March 12, 2018, https://entreatingfavor.com/biblical-repentance/.

9 Whenever Paul speaks of a good desire in the NT, (as he does thirteen times) he uses this Greek word *zelos* that is translated as longing. Conversely when he speaks of a wrong, lustful desire he uses *epithymia*.

10 John Murray, *Redemption Accomplished and Applied* (Grand Rapids: Eerdmans, 2015), 106.

11 Hughes, *The New International Commentary*.

12 John MacArthur, *The MacArthur Study Bible* (Nashville: W Publishing Group, 1997).

If I speak with the tongues of men and of angels, but do not have love, I have become a noisy gong or a clanging cymbal. If I have the gift of prophecy, and know all mysteries and all knowledge; and if I have all faith, so as to remove mountains, but do not have love, I am nothing. And if I give all my possessions to feed the poor, and if I surrender my body to be burned, but do not have love, it profits me nothing.

Love is patient, love is kind and is not jealous; love does not brag and is not arrogant, does not act unbecomingly; it does not seek its own, is not provoked, does not take into account a wrong suffered, does not rejoice in unrighteousness, but rejoices with the truth; bears all things, believes all things, hopes all things, endures all things.

Love never fails; but if there are gifts of prophecy, they will be done away; if there are tongues, they will cease; if there is knowledge, it will be done away. For we know in part and we prophesy in part; but when the perfect comes, the partial will be done away. When I was a child, I used to speak like a child, think like a child, reason like a child; when I became a man, I did away with childish things. For now we see in a mirror dimly, but then face to face; now I know in part, but then I will know fully just as I also have been fully known. But now faith, hope, love, abide these three; but the greatest of these is love.

1 CORINTHIANS 13

CHAPTER 6

The Preeminence of Love

Without love as the central feature of your faith, your influence in office will be less than it could be. Your spouse, family members, and colleagues must know in their heart of hearts that you are first and foremost a loving person in order for you to be influential. As Paul states, without love "*I am nothing*." What then are the defining aspects of love that we need to be continually working on and growing in?

Chapter 13 of 1 Corinthians is sandwiched between two chapters of instruction by Paul to the church at Corinth, whose members, in their carnality, emphasize the practice of certain spiritual gifts above the practice of Christian love. Paul instructs them that love is preeminent—it's what ties people together.

We will be looking at fifteen love-defining words, all of which are presented in the present continuous tense, "denoting actions and attitudes which have become habitual, ingrained gradually by constant repetition."[1] The defining characteristics of love are worthy of constant review and practice with our spouses, family members, office staff, and professional colleagues. Love is what ties us together and sustains our relationships.

Given that repetition is the key to learning and ingraining, I like to study the topic of love often. Akin to driving a car, these specific, measurable aspects of love should become habitual responses in our lives, even though they are more difficult and take much longer to cultivate than the rote habits of driving a car.

Before examining the fundamental elements of love, Paul first emphasizes—and appropriately so—the *essentiality* of love as the superior trait. Let's look at that first.

The Essentiality of Love: 1 Corinthians 13:1–3

> *If I speak with the tongues of men and of angels, but do not have love, I have become a noisy gong or a clanging cymbal. If I have the gift of prophecy, and know all mysteries and all knowledge; and if I have all faith, so as to remove mountains, but do not have love, I am nothing. And if I give all my possessions to feed the poor, and if I surrender my body to be burned, but do not have love, it profits me nothing.*

In these three opening verses, Paul makes three stark comparisons in order to underscore the incomparability of *love*. These introductory remarks exclaim the dominance of love as a virtue over all other character traits. It is important, motivating, and insightful to note that the three comparisons are related to qualities necessary to succeed in the Capital Community: one must possess speaking skills (v. 1), leadership (v. 2), and self-sacrifice (v. 3). As critical as those are, from God's perspective, love is of even greater importance!

Let's elaborate on each of Paul's comparisons. The first in verse 1 pertains to a person's oratory abilities.

LOVE OVER ORATION: 1 CORINTHIANS 13:1

> *If I speak with the tongues of men and of angels, but do not have love, I have become a noisy gong or a clanging cymbal.*

Your *love* for others is more important than your speaking abilities. The metaphorical meaning of becoming "*a noisy gong or a clanging cymbal*" relates to empty philosophizing. Someone who knows and exclaims all the right answers but has no love is akin to the church of Ephesus as described in Revelation 2:1–7. That church has all the right doctrine but has lost their love for God. Proverbs 3:3 summarizes the necessary virtues of a Public Servant as both a herald of truth and a man or woman of love: "*Do not let kindness and truth leave you; Bind them around your neck, Write them on the tablet of your heart.*" Solomon's use of the words *neck* and *heart* bespeak both *love* (kindness) and *truth* as being a part of one's outward and inward adornment. The meaning of the Hebrew word for "heart" (*leb*) includes the aspects of one's intellect, emotion, and will. The mature believer possesses both love and truth in full measure.

Because their priorities are straight, Public Servants who are loving are neither inwardly nor outwardly "*a noisy gong or a clanging cymbal.*" Even when they herald the truth in public debate, their speech is couched in words of love.

LOVE OVER LEADING: 1 CORINTHIANS 13:2

> If I have the gift of prophecy, and know all mysteries and all knowledge; and if I have all faith, so as to remove mountains, but do not have love, I am nothing.

It is not a stretch to interpret the second verse of chapter 13 as a statement of the primacy of love over leadership. Public Servants who know the Word of God, who are *knowledgeable* of all the policy issues, and possess *faith*—i.e., visionary leadership for the future—but do not possess a genuine, heart-felt *love* for people, amount to *nothing*, Scripture tells us. The phrase "*so as to remove mountains*" is Pauline hyperbole[2] (also seen in v. 7) intended to convey, "to make what seems impossible possible."[3] You may be a great leader or an up-and-coming great leader in American government, one who may be able to achieve what others deem impossible. You may be a person of great faith, but never forget that it is more important to love people—especially those who have nothing to do with helping you accomplish your leadership objectives. Don't kid yourself into thinking that people don't pick up on self-centeredness.

How to Become a Marginalized Public Servant

In my years of ministry in the California State Capitol building, and since 2010 in the U.S. Capitol, I have observed certain Members who became marginalized, ineffective, and discounted by others because they doubled down on truth at the expense of love. I beg you not to follow in their footsteps. It is essential that you are as loving as you are truthful!

LOVE OVER SELF-SACRIFICE: 1 CORINTHIANS 13:3

And if I give all my possessions to feed the poor, and if I surrender my body to be burned, but do not have love, it profits me nothing.

To be sure, those who *give* sacrificially of time, talent, and treasure are to be respected above those who do not. But compared to love, sacrificial qualities are of lesser significance. In fact, a life of personal sacrifice for whatever objectives wanes in comparison to a life of loving others. One who lacks love is woefully deficient.

"Love is the indispensable addition which alone gives worth to all other Christian gifts."[4]

Lord, help us to work on being more loving! Life in the Capital, in the community, or in the home without love is "nothing" (*oudeis*). How are you doing as a preeminently loving person—a lover of people, and especially your spouse if you are married? Keep in mind that emotions, both good and bad, always stem from one's thinking, either proper or improper. We have control over our thoughts, as we submit to the process of having our minds renewed in Jesus (Romans 12:2).

What follows the *essentiality* of love in the inspired mind of the apostle Paul is the objective *evidence* of love; it should help to answer the question, "Am I a loving person?" Evidence of love supersedes subjective feelings that may or may not accurately reflect one's real love quotient.

The Evidence of Love: 1 Corinthians 13:4–7

Love is patient, love is kind and is not jealous; love does not brag and is not arrogant, does not act unbecomingly; it does not seek its own, is not provoked, does not take into account a wrong suffered, does not rejoice in unrighteousness, but rejoices with the truth; bears all things, believes all things, hopes all things, endures all things.

Love is an often-misused word with a broad array of definitions in our culture. With the Scripture as our guide we can zero in on the truth about love. Paul opens by stating what love is: *love is patient* and *kind*. Paul then describes seven characteristics of love's absence—what love is *not*. Sometimes the best way to describe what something is, is to state what it's not.

LOVE IS PATIENT (*MAKROTHUMEO*)

Literally *longsuffering*. This first characteristic of love is the ability to be taken advantage of by a person many times and not be upset. The root word means "to persevere." James uses this same Greek word in describing the attitude of the prophets of old whose words went unheeded by their peers (cf. James 5:8ff.). Program your mind with Philippians 1:6:

> *For I am confident of this very thing, that He who began a good work in you will perfect it until the day of Christ Jesus.*

The truth of this passage will help sober you to the fact that God is not through sanctifying the offending person—in fact, *none of us is perfect*! So be *patient*, not condemning and judgmental! Remember too that since Christ forgave your sins—past, present, and future—you must find room in your heart to forgive others who have wronged you. To be longsuffering, or patient, with another's shortcomings is to be categorically loving!

LOVE IS KIND (*CHRESTEUOMAI*)

The counterpart of patience is *kindness*. The Greek word means "to show oneself mild." This characteristic is shown in a willingness to give to another, including one's enemies, and to be gentle and slow in avenging. The Greek root speaks to one desires and works for another's welfare. It is the idea of good will, generous responses and actions, in contradistinction to holding onto past bad memories and being continually bothered (as in, "He gets on my nerves").

LOVE IS NOT JEALOUS (*ZELOO*)

At its root, being *jealous* means to "desire earnestly." Jealousy as it is used here is similar to covetousness, carrying the idea of envy. It is a desire to have what another possesses, as well as fearing that someone will take what you have. In contrast, Scripture commands us not to want what others possess, and to give to others what we possess. We are to "*rejoice with those who rejoice*" (Romans 12:15). Choose to be glad for those who have—be they more talented, successful, popular, or beautiful—rather than being jealous or envious. Are you the biggest cheerleader of your mate, children, grandchildren, and colleagues?

LOVE DOES NOT BRAG (*PERPEREUOMAI*)

Literally "to boast or vaunt oneself." The mature in Christ has forgotten about self-importance. Center on others, not self. Proverbs 27:2 states:

Let another praise you, and not your own mouth; A stranger, and not your own lips.

Further, be known for asking sincere questions. Cultivate personal curiosity, talking little about yourself. Don't be quick to add your personal stories to every conversation. In the crowds in which you circulate, everyone already gets the point; they don't need to hear your long-winded illustrations that include individuals they know nothing about. It is better to spend your time asking questions of others and giving short answers when asked a question. *Love does not brag.* When approaching a conversation, ask yourself, "What can I learn from this person?" versus "What can I tell them about me?"

LOVE IS NOT ARROGANT (*PHUSIOO*)

Literally "to puff or blow up." William Carey, who translated the Bible into thirty-four languages, was once insulted at a banquet. An arrogant man said to him, "Mr. Carey, I understand that you were once a shoemaker." Carey replied, "I was not a shoemaker, only a shoe repairman!"[5] Strive to be bighearted, not bigheaded. Make it a habit to downplay self in the presence of others. Proverbs 16:18 states:

Pride goes before destruction, And a haughty spirit before stumbling.

Conversely, keep in mind James 4:6:

God ... gives grace to the humble.

LOVE DOES NOT ACT UNBECOMINGLY (*ASCHEMONEO*)

This is the characteristic of those who care so little for others around them that they act without proper decorum for the occasion. They act rudely or impolitely, maybe even crudely. Work always on sensitivity toward others. Always display respect for another regardless of their position or ability to assist in your objectives.

LOVE DOES NOT SEEK ITS OWN (*ZETEO HEAUTOU*)

Jesus "*did not come to be served, but to serve*" (Matthew 20:28). Be occupied with others' needs, not your own. Philippians 2:3 states:

Do nothing from selfishness or empty conceit, but with humility of mind regard one another as more important than yourselves.

This is boilerplate Christianity! Are your spouse's or colleagues' objectives *more important* to you than your own? What will you give by way of time, talent, and treasure for your spouse or colleague that will demonstrate unmistakably that you cherish them above *yourself*?

One of the measurable aspects of love is not seeking your self-interests all the time. Coach Wooden used to stress the habit of doing a daily kind deed for someone who in no way can repay you. That is an excellent habit because it keeps reminding us of this truth: *Love does not seek its own.*

LOVE IS NOT PROVOKED (*PAROXUNO*)

Literally "to irritate, arouse to anger." Love guards against being upset, irritated, or angered. Remember, love is kind. People who are intent on having their own way are easily *provoked* when they don't get what they want.[6]

LOVE DOES NOT TAKE INTO ACCOUNT A WRONG SUFFERED (*LOGIZOMAI*)

The Greek has the idea of not "ledgering," or keeping a running log, of the *wrongs* done against you. On the contrary:

> An important early church father, Chrysostom, remarked that a wrong done against love is like a spark that falls into the sea and is extinguished forever.

The famous saying "Don't get mad, get even" illustrates the opposite of the idea being conveyed here. If you are a Christian, your response must be to forgive and forget. You are to obliterate the memory of wrongs done to you, rather than hanging on to them. Do not cultivate a memory akin to an elephant. Praise God that He doesn't take into consideration our past sin! Clasping onto the virtue of Christ's forgiveness enables us to forsake the bondage of bitterness. Don't keep a log—it is not loving. Paul, who was more ill-treated than you will ever be, said, *"forgetting what lies behind"* (Philippians 3:13). Can the same be said of you? Do you instead *"press on toward the goal for the prize of the upward call of God in Christ Jesus"* (Philippians 3:14)?

LOVE DOES NOT REJOICE IN UNRIGHTEOUSNESS (*ADIKIA*)

Isaiah warns, *"Woe to those who call evil good, and good evil"* (Isaiah 5:20). It is not loving to sacrifice truth. One should not applaud the presence of sin in another. The Biblical concept of love is not emotional sentimentality devoid of truth.

LOVE REJOICES WITH THE TRUTH (*ALETHEIA*)

Love cares that what another believes is *truthful*. It is not loving to allow others to be hurt by lies, since what they believe and then act upon can determine personal, family, and national destinies. Love does not *rejoice* with erroneous thinking.[7]

The following remaining four elements of love are expressed by means of a literary device known as *hyperbole*: exaggeration in order to make a strong point. (See fn2). The repetition of "*all things*" in the following passages refers to everything within the confines of God's righteousness, will, and tolerance.

LOVE BEARS ALL THINGS (*STEGO*)

Literally "to cover." In other words, "*Love covers a multitude of sins*" (1 Peter 4:8; cf. Proverbs 10:12). You can measure your love for another by how quickly you are willing to forgive and forget their faults and move on.

The believer's actions must emulate God's character as revealed in Psalm 103:12:

> *As far as the east is from the west, So far has He removed our transgressions from us.*

In order for us to be as loving as Jesus expects us to be, we must forgive and forget.

LOVE BELIEVES ALL THINGS (*PISTEUO*)

Love trusts; it is confident. It isn't suspicious or cynical. Love trusts even after having been hurt from trusting in the past. It is better to trust and be hurt again than to end up living life alone and embittered. Keep taking risks in your relationships!

LOVE HOPES ALL THINGS (*ELPIZO*)

This relates to "happy anticipation." Jesus did not take Peter's failure as final. The believer continues to *hope* that sinners will someday turn from their sin and that believers will continually mature in Christ, for to lose hope is equivalent to losing love. Again, as with the virtue of patience, "*I am confident of this very thing, that He who began a good work in you will perfect it until the day of Christ Jesus*," states Paul in Philippians 1:6. Remember, as long as God's grace remains operational in this world, human failure is never final. People can learn from their mistakes. Hope for the best in people—to carry within you such an optimistic attitude toward others is to be loving!

LOVE ENDURES ALL THINGS (*HUPOMENO*)

This Greek word is used of an army that holds its position no matter what the cost. Love holds fast to the one it loves. It will stand against all opposition. Love remains loyal even when the object of love is less than perfect.

These fifteen virtues may seem somewhat mechanical, but they will produce the critically important love that ties us together for the long run!

Theologically speaking, all of these attributes of love already perfectly exist in the child of God, according to Colossians 2:10a. The believer is made perfect before God at the point of salvation. How close we are to our new God-given, perfectly loving nature in everyday practice is a matter of obedience. No believer can reason, "I am just not a very loving person." All believers are perfect in love. The question is how obedient are we to our new nature in Christ?

The Exuberance of Love

Let us briefly review Colossians 3:12–14 for additional insights into the emotional aspects of love. This passage speaks of the passions of love:

> *So, as those who have been chosen of God, holy and beloved, put on a heart of compassion, kindness, humility, gentleness and patience; bearing with one another, and forgiving each other, whoever has a complaint against anyone; just as the Lord forgave you, so also should you. Beyond all these things, put on love, which is the perfect bond of unity.*

In light of all the perfect sacrificial love Jesus Christ has displayed to and for the world (John 3:16), God expects nothing less in response from His followers.

HEART OF COMPASSION (*SPLAGCHNON OIKTIRMOS*)

This speaks of the seat of emotions. The elements that follow in this passage are very similar to the ones in 1

Corinthians 13, but are listed here in the context of having a *heart of compassion*.

> ## God's exuberant, supernatural love is poured forth in the life of the believer through the indwelling Holy Spirit.

Again and importantly, all of the elements of love presently exist in the believer's heart (cf. Ephesians 1:3; Colossians 2:10; 2 Peter 1:3–4). It isn't a matter of gaining them; it is a matter of taking ownership and using them!

The aspects of love listed in Corinthians and Colossians are all characteristics of the truly redeemed, and they should naturally flow forth in and from the life of every Spirit-filled follower of Christ!

The Eternality of Love

Returning to the closing passages on love found in 1 Corinthians 13, we read:

LOVE NEVER FAILS

Love is permanent. It is an attribute of God, which means it never withers or decays. It is not as if love is important to one generation and not another. Love is to be present and active in the life of every believer at all times and in every generation. Like Jesus, we must possess eternal, unfailing, ever-present love! Godly (*agape*) love is part of the believer's very nature! May these virtues of love increasingly unfold for you! May you conscientiously and habitually cultivate Christ's unending love in your life!

May God help you to put on the very nature every believer already possesses, reflecting love's *essentiality* as the superior trait, showing *evidence* of love in your life, expressing love's *exuberance*, and entering into God's *eternal* mission of love. Amen!

What happens to the pursuit of knowledge in the life of the believer who is wholeheartedly endeavoring to express the love of God? Do those two pursuits conflict with one another? We will now address that question as we look at the role of knowledge in our Christian walk.

Notes

1 David Prior, *The Message of 1 Corinthians* (Nottingham, England: Inter-Varsity Press, 1985), 229–30.

2 In the literary genres of Scripture, as in the best of writing today, various figurative devices are utilized to communicate effectively and artfully. These devices (among many) include simile, allegory, ellipsis, metaphor, paradox, irony, and euphemisms. The figurative device used by Paul in 1 Corinthians 13:2 & 7 is hyperbole. The people of the Middle East in ancient times used exaggerated expressions to convey a thought with more force. An additional example would be what the apostle John states in his Gospel about recording the events in the life of Christ: "*I suppose that even the world itself would not contain the books that would be written*" (John 21:25). (cf. E. W. Bullinger, *Figures of Speech Used in the Bible* [London: Messrs, Eyre, & Spottiswoode, 1889], 171ff.) Such insights defy a wooden, literalistic approach (of which evangelicals are often falsely accused) to Biblical interpretation/hermeneutics.

3 H. L. Strack and P. Billerbeck, *Kommentar zum Neuen Testament aus Talmud und Midrasch*, 1922–1928. As quoted in C. K. Barrett, *The First Epistle To The Corinthians, Blacks New Testament Commentary Series* (London: Hendrickson, 1968), 301.

4 Ibid., 303. This quote brings together chapters 12 and 14.

5 Joseph Randall, "May God Grant More Humility!," April 8, 2009, *Feeding on Christ*, accessed March 12, 2018, http://feedingonchrist.com/may-god-grant-more-humility/.

6 The exception to not being provoked is if another is maligning or contradicting God's Word. Being provoked over such can be understood as righteous indignation.

7 Here Biblical Christianity conflicts with postmodernism in that the Christian faith is based upon moral absolutes as explicated in and through propositional truth, i.e., infallible and inerrant Biblical revelation.

Incline your ear and hear the words of the wise,
And apply your mind to my knowledge;
For it will be pleasant if you keep them within you,
That they may be ready on your lips.

PROVERBS 22:17–18

CHAPTER 7

The Essentiality of Knowledge

Scripture is replete with verses that emphasize how the believer must be characterized first and foremost by love. Love is essential and preeminent! But a close second is the believer's lifetime pursuit of knowledge. In fact, Proverbs calls those who are lacking in knowledge simpletons, whereas those who have knowledge are called wise.

As a Public Servant, one must not be unloving, or a simpleton, in order to be a good witness for Christ, as well as be effective in office. Now we will examine the importance of the pursuit of knowledge in the life of the believer.

The primacy of love over knowledge is underscored in 1 Corinthians 13:1, where the great apostle states, *"If I speak with the tongues of men and of angels, but do not have love, I have become a noisy gong or a clanging cymbal."* Elsewhere, in 1 Corinthians 8:1, Paul makes a similar comparison when he states, *"Knowledge puffs up, but love edifies"* (NKJV). To be sure, *knowledge* as a pursuit of one's life should take a back seat to the priority of *love*. Loving our Savior and loving others must be the primary pursuit of the believer's life. But having said that, the pursuit of knowledge is not in any way inconsistent with a life devoted to love—they are two facets of the same jewel.

The False Dichotomy between Love and Knowledge

An important clarification is in order regarding a perceived tension between love and knowledge. In stating the preeminence of love over knowledge, it is improper to assert that someone who pursues knowledge is somehow less than loving. To diminish knowledge as an element of spiritual maturity in favor of just being loving is a misreading of God's priorities. In fact, someone recently told me he thought that one of America's greatest theologically conservative seminaries was more of a "cemetery" than a "seminary," as if its focus on knowledge was at the expense of love. Such thinking reflects a tragic mindset that is increasing in American Christianity today. To illustrate this point metaphorically:

> ## Can you say that someone who eats an enormous breakfast each morning is an overeater, when he is preparing to compete in the Tour de France?

In a spiritual sense, mental preparedness, or gaining knowledge, is essential for any important Kingdom assignment, such as serving Christ in city, county, state, or national government. In fact, nutrition is a prerequisite for performing with excellence. So don't be misled by those who would have you diminish your pursuit of the nourishment of knowledge, especially knowledge of God's ways through His Word! The believer in office, like any citizen, can be both knowledgeable and loving at the same time. Those who pursue knowledge are not necessarily unloving; to propose such a notion is to propagate a false dichotomy.

The Underlying Motives for Gaining Knowledge

What is the motive behind your pursuit of knowledge? As previously stated from 1 Corinthians 8:1, knowledge can puff up, meaning it can be the pursuit of a proud heart in order to show oneself superior. Or the pursuit of knowledge can be equivalent to seeking mental preparedness.

In the book of Proverbs, the word *knowledge* appears forty times, and is always related to and descriptive of a wise person. Shunning knowledge is also discussed. In Proverbs 1:22 the personified voice of wisdom speaks:

> *"How long, O naïve ones, will you love being simple-minded? And scoffers delight themselves in scoffing And fools hate knowledge?"*

Again in Proverbs 1:28–29 wisdom speaks of knowledge as equated with fear of the Lord:

> *"Then they will call on me, but I will not answer; They will seek me diligently but they will not find me, Because they hated knowledge And did not choose the fear of the LORD."*

The underlying motive for gaining knowledge is often a determining factor of whether or not it is a holy pursuit. If one possesses the right spirit of glorifying God, building His Kingdom, winning the lost to Christ, and being a preserver and illuminator in culture, then the quest for knowledge is undoubtedly a wonderful thing that is both God honoring and God blessed!

Spiritual Growth Is Dependent on Knowledge

Perhaps the most powerful way to illustrate that one's faith in Christ must be cognitive as well as loving is to examine the three Biblically identified stages of the believer's spiritual growth as listed in 1 John 2:12–14. This passage illustrates the proposition that knowledge is extremely important to the Christian's life and growth. In fact, without the pursuit of Biblical knowledge there will be no maturation in Christ. Carefully observe how each of the following stages of spiritual growth is dependent on knowledge.

SUMMARY OVERVIEW OF 1 JOHN 2:12–14

> *I am writing to you, little children, because your sins have been forgiven you for His name's sake. I am writing to you, fathers, because you know Him who has been from the beginning. I am writing to you, young men, because you have overcome the evil one. I have written to you, children, because you know the Father. I have written to you, fathers, because you know Him who has been from the beginning. I have written to you, young men, because you are strong, and the word of God abides in you, and you have overcome the evil one.*

The chart below is an attempt to sort out the three distinct stages of spiritual maturity as delineated and repeated by the apostle John in this passage. Observe the titles with which John identifies each stage: little children, fathers, and young men. Think of John's communication style here as painting a wall with two separate coats in order to obtain the desired richness of color.

THE THREE STAGES OF SPIRITUAL GROWTH IN CHRIST: 1 JOHN 2:12–14

STAGE	CHARACTERISTICS	VERSE
Little Children	Sins forgiven	12
	Knowledge of the Father	13
Young Men	Have overcome the evil one	13
	Strong	14
	Word of God abides in you	
	Have overcome the evil one	
Fathers	Knowledge of Him	13
	Knowledge of Him from the beginning	14

In John's analogy of physical maturation to spiritual maturation, the Greek words used to describe the believers' stages of growth are not intended to relate to their physical age, but rather their level of spiritual maturity. Each of these stages of spiritual growth relates to the pursuit of knowledge! With this in mind, let's look more closely at each of the three.

LITTLE CHILDREN OF THE FAITH

Little children are saved. Their sins have been forgiven, but they only possess a rudimentary understanding of God. "Jesus loves me this I know, for the Bible tells me so!" perfectly expresses their level of understanding of salvation; they possess little knowledge of Biblical doctrine. Nonetheless, they possess enough Biblical knowledge to be genuinely saved, in comparison to an unsaved person, whose sins have not been forgiven, and who does not possess any saving knowledge.

Satan can and often does make havoc of little children
because they have little knowledge of his wiles.

Christian cults often target little children in the faith because they are tenderhearted toward spiritual matters, but very naïve; Ephesians 4:14 describes and admonishes infant believers:

> *As a result, we are no longer to be children, tossed here and there by waves and carried about by every wind of doctrine, by the trickery of men, by craftiness in deceitful scheming.*

Spiritual babes, this passage states, should not remain in such a state of infancy. They should not remain naïve, or unknowledgeable of the *winds*, *trickery*, and *craftiness* that have the potential to make them highly unstable as newborn babes in Christ. In opposition to those who say that knowledge in the life of the believer is unimportant or of lessor importance, this passage suggests the opposite is true. Scripture says knowledge is absolutely critical to spiritual maturity!

YOUNG MEN OF THE FAITH

Young men are those who, while not yet having walked with God for a long period of time, do know sound doctrine, in contrast with the child who does not. Young men are strong against sin and error because "*the word of God abides*" in them, which is synonymous with having knowledge of His Word. As we see from the description of young men in this passage, through their knowledge they have been made strong to overcome the deceitfulness of the evil one.

FATHERS OF THE FAITH

The father of the faith is the one whom John depicts as the most spiritually mature; he has a deep, abiding knowledge of the eternal God. Twice John states that the father "*knows Him*." A father has experienced the truths of His Word first-hand. This is consistent with Philippians 3:10 where the apostle Paul, a father of the faith, states regarding himself, "*that I may know Him*." The height of spiritual maturity is to *know* God in His fullness through His Word and the first-hand knowledge of having experienced the truths of His Word in one's life.

Summary of the Three Stages of Spiritual Growth

All three of the stages of spiritual growth are related to knowledge. One can only become a father in the faith by first becoming a believer, starting out as a little child. The little child then graduates to become a young man by being strong in the Word, which implies obtaining knowledge. As the young man grows in knowledge and first-hand experience of the truth of God's Word, he becomes a father in the faith. Proverbs 22:17 is a fitting summation: "*Apply your mind to my knowledge.*"

Herein lies the Biblical case for the noble pursuit of knowledge in a nutshell: pursuing knowledge is tantamount to spiritual maturation and God's glorification! Biblical knowledge is foundational to the life of every believer and especially those who serve in leadership.

Proverbs 3:3 states very fittingly that both knowledge and love are essential to the life of the believer:

Do not let kindness and truth leave you; Bind them around your neck, Write them on the tablet of your heart.

Don't let anyone lead you into thinking that the Christian life does not include a hearty pursuit of knowledge; as if the pursuit of God's Word is less than spiritual. The opposite is true.

We have begun to look at the role our faith can play in government leadership. We've identified some key ingredients for effective service and personal growth, including love and knowledge. Now let's dig a little deeper and ask, on what foundation is our knowledge based? What presuppositions guide our thinking? What are the consequences for us if we acknowledge the authority of Scripture, and likewise, if we do not?

THERE ARE MORE THAN FOUR HUNDRED SPECIES OF OAK TREES, and some of them reach heights of one hundred feet and live for hundreds—some think thousands—of years. Fortified by a stalwart root system that it spent years and most of its energy building, the oak tree's strong, sinuous branches can spread even wider, reaching widths of up to 120 feet. Those stately branches provide ample shade and shelter for wildlife. Leaves and twigs are nest-building materials for the homes of robins, blue jays, starlings, squirrels, raccoons, and opossums that the oak cradles in its branches. White oak acorns germinate shortly after falling, while the acorns from red oaks lie dormant for months, providing food for wildlife in winter and into spring. The oak absorbs carbon dioxide through its leaves, extracts the carbon, which fosters its growth, and then releases oxygen through its leaves. In one day a large oak can provide enough oxygen for four people; it can lift up to one hundred gallons of water out of the ground and discharge it into the air.

PART II

SCRIPTURAL AUTHORITY

We are destroying speculations and every lofty thing raised up against the knowledge of God, and we are taking every thought captive to the obedience of Christ.

2 CORINTHIANS 10:5

CHAPTER 8

Understanding Epistemological Presuppositions

Epistemology is "the branch of philosophy that examines the nature of knowledge, its presuppositions and foundations, and its extent and validity."[1]. I like what Merriam-Webster adds in the formation of a working definition: "The study or a theory of the nature and grounds of knowledge especially with reference to its limits and validity."[2] It is extremely important to take time to consider the limitations and validity of our sources of knowledge, and what we deem authoritative. The study of epistemology uncovers what we rely on and what informs our thinking about right and wrong. Are our presuppositions valid? As we get older we subconsciously rely on our ingrained epistemological habits; we assume their validity. But again, are they right?

Wise are those who can discern not only their own, but others' epistemological presuppositions, or assumptions. Wise are the citizens who can discern a candidate's epistemological presuppositions before casting their ballots. Heightening our awareness regarding starting points of thought is what this chapter is all about.

Epistemology is closely related to *ontology*. Whereas epistemology asks questions about the origins and validity of knowledge, ontology asks questions about the nature and origin of being. Both philosophical disciplines attempt to address and study these basic issues regarding life on earth: "Why do I exist and what should inform my beliefs?"

Christians answer those questions with the presupposition that Scripture is the final authority; the Bible informs their thinking regarding epistemological and ontological concerns. On the other hand, secularists are informed by other sources. Our presuppositions—i.e., what we utilize to formulate our answers in relation to these two disciplines—are many and varied. For instance, many people rely either consciously or unconsciously on the values they learned in their upbringing as the final authority in their life decisions. Others rely on their experiences or present circumstances, i.e., the presenting situation. Still others are guided by the ideology of their teachers and professors, or the books they have read.

Therefore, wise are those who are not blind to their own and others' presuppositions in life. What informs our thinking? What determines our actions?

> To think through issues with curiosity, and to root out their epistemological basis is to be discerning and wise.

This is critically important, especially where the future course of a nation is at stake. I like the New Living Translation of Proverbs 14:15, in which one who does not discern epistemologically is called a *simpleton*. *"Only simpletons believe everything they're told! The prudent carefully consider their steps"* (Proverbs 14:15 NLT). Discipline yourself to be a deep and discerning thinker, not a *simpleton*!

Contrasting Valid and Invalid Presuppositions

Healthy growing Christians are conscientiously *putting off* and *putting on*. They are leaving behind invalid and limited epistemological presuppositions, and in their place they are reprogramming with a Biblical epistemology. Note this in Ephesians 4:22–25a:

In reference to your former manner of life, you lay aside the old self, which is being corrupted in accordance with the lusts of deceit, and that you be renewed in the spirit of your mind, and put on the new self, which in the likeness of God has been created in righteousness and holiness of the truth. Therefore laying aside falsehood, SPEAK TRUTH EACH ONE of you.

This growth process is consistent with what Paul tells the worldly believers in Corinth. In 2 Corinthians 10:5 the apostle states:

We are destroying speculations and every lofty thing raised up against the knowledge of God, and we are taking every thought captive to the obedience of Christ.

This passage arises from the same context of Paul's earlier pronouncements regarding the fallacy of human reasoning apart from divine revelation (cf. 1 Corinthians 1:18–25; Job 5:13; Psalm 94:11). The word *speculations* carries with it the idea of the world's ways of reasoning, its philosophies, and its false religions. These mental bombardments are attempts by the evil one to block seekers of truth from the witness of their consciences and the ever-beckoning call of the Gospel of Christ. In short, it is normative behavior in a godless world. The expectation of God is that His called-out representatives will zero in exclusively on a Biblical epistemology, forsaking all other presuppositions of truth. Every way of thinking must be brought "*captive to the obedience of Christ.*"

THE ROLE OF FAITH IN PRESUPPOSITIONS

All people hold their starting points of reasoning—or presuppositions regarding what is right and wrong—to be authoritative *by faith*. They accept by faith the validity and authority of their parents, professors, favorite authors, life experience, or in the case of the Christian, the revelation of Scripture. This is an important distinction to make up front because in the illustrations that follow we will see that non-believers will deny that faith is a starting point for their own belief systems, in a game of one-upmanship.

TRUTH FROM THE INSIDE

Two additional epistemological starting points that take us a step further are called *rationalism* and *empiricism*. Rationalism begins with reasoning by the use of deduction and logic. Empiricism calls on our senses to gather knowledge and information experientially to determine what is right or wrong. What these two views have in common is the assumption (by faith I might add) that the human mind alone can be relied upon to discern truth from falsehood. This is a huge presupposition! By contrast, the Christian believes:

Truth originates not in the human mind, but in the mind of God, and is revealed to us through the Bible.

The presupposition of the believer is that the human mind is biased toward sin and given to irrationality and partiality due to the fall of man in Genesis 3. In that the fall affected man's ability to think truthfully at all times—theologically this is called the *noetic* effect of sin—the human mind is not a trustworthy starting point. To hold to an epistemology that assumes that moral truth can be determined by the use of one's sensory perceptions is to work in a contaminated laboratory. The Bible says we cannot trust ourselves to come up with the right answers. In other words, absolute truth cannot be derived from a secular humanist epistemology. In fact, the closer the matter gets to the eternal moral truths that have their origin in God, the more biased the fallen human mind becomes.

TRUTH FROM THE OUTSIDE

The testimony of Scripture is this: the fallen sin nature of humanity requires that we derive truth from outside ourselves—from an external epistemological source untainted by our defective human reasoning. Both Jesus Christ and the Scriptures are testimony to that. God has revealed His plan to us not only through His incarnate Son, but through the external, objective written source that is untainted by sin, called the Bible. In this way He purely communicates the message of redemption and objectively conveys truth throughout the course of time.

It follows then that the study of God's revelation in the Bible allows for certainty of truth, right thinking, and the basis for proper ontological understanding. This is not limited to matters of political import and candidates, but is the starting point for discerning no less than one's very purpose in life.

Rejected by the unregenerate and embraced by the believer, the Bible is the only reliable and certain epistemology in the universe; all other sources are tainted to some degree by the bias of endemic sin. Furthermore, the alternative is to exalt one's opinions over and above the authoritative teachings of the Bible. Of course, self-authority is the popular trend, and one does not have to look very far to see it playing out in American culture. An example of secularists' epistemological hubris is their reaction to Chick-fil-A CEO Daniel Cathy's stand on God's definition of marriage.

Secularists loudly assert in their latest cause du jour that they are morally superior to Biblical authority, saying in essence, "We have a better understanding of marriage than God does." The problem is that unbelievers, whose reasoning flies in the face of divine revelation, face the daunting task of proving that their beliefs have a stronger, more reliable basis than the Word of God. What is the presupposition that informs their opinion? Is it not subjective?

TRUTH PERSONIFIED

We have seen that truth comes from an external, untainted source: Notice what Jesus adds to this understanding in John 14:6:

> *"I am the way, and the truth, and the life."*

The Scriptures not only proclaim that the certitude of absolute, authoritative *truth* is found outside of fallen man, but that Jesus Himself is the personification of truth. In other words, since one of the attributes of God is truth, one must accept that God not only knows the truth, but is truth; therefore to reject God is to reject truth.

CIRCULAR REASONING

We have discussed how all epistemological assumptions are held by faith. That means that every argument is circular in nature. The fact that Christians use the Bible to uphold their premise that the Bible is God's Word is no different from the evolutionists using fossil evidence to support their worldview. Whereas the theory is informed by the source, the theory also informs the source. Why then should one understand the Christian's epistemology to be superior? It is for this reason:

In direct contrast to Christianity's theistic *intervention* is humanistic *invention*. Whereas the former is imported from *outside* the human mind, the latter is manufactured from *within*. This stark difference must be emphasized by the Christian apologist. In other words, by way of cogent argumentation, unbelievers must come to see the absurdity of their epistemology. Humanism is a belief informed by *internal estimation*—the fallible mind of man, whereas ours is a belief informed by *external revelation*—the infallible mind of God. For this reason, the believer's starting point, or presupposition—is superior. In essence, it's not all about me, it's all about God.

Illustrating Valid and Invalid Presuppositions

In order to bring a better working understanding of this concept, a narrative illustration is in order.

DONAHUE AND MOHLER

Years ago Dr. Albert Mohler debated Phil Donahue on the latter's television program. Dr. Mohler is the dean of a leading evangelical seminary. Donahue pressed Mohler regarding the justice of a Nazi murdering a Jew, the Jew going to hell, and the possibility that the Nazi might go on to obtain Christian salvation. Rather than allow Donahue's reasoning to place Mohler on the defensive, in my humble opinion Mohler should have challenged Donahue regarding the epistemological basis for his assumption that murder is wrong in the first place! What basis of authority did Donahue start from in assuming that murder is wrong? Is it not the case that Donahue borrowed from Mohler's Scriptural presuppositions in formulating his charge of divine injustice (while arrogantly implying that he was more fair-minded than God)? Had I been in Mohler's position (and without all the pressure of live TV) I would have said, "It's obvious from your statement that you believe murder to be wrong. That is certainly my position, but what is your basis of authority to conclude that murder is wrong?" Donahue was clearly borrowing principles from Mohler's playbook without attribution, while simultaneously questioning the validity of the Author of his source Book! Donahue can't have it both ways. Such hypocrisy should have been brought to the surface.

Properly and lovingly interrogated, Donahue would have had to admit that he believed murder was wrong based on his own thinking. The humanist will typically attempt to counter this conclusion with "everyone thinks murder is wrong, therefore it is wrong," which can be summarized as an argument from convention. The problem with postulating an argument from convention is that not everyone believes murder is wrong—witness ISIS and of course Adolph Hitler. So then what is Donahue's basis of authority other than his own thinking?

Apart from the Scriptures, Donahue possessed no moral authority other than his personal opinion to wage his attack on Mohler. Mohler could have carried the day had he stated that Donahue's morality was a matter of his own interpretation to begin with. Unless one borrows from the presupposition of Scripture's teaching, i.e., in this case, *"You shall not murder,"* one can only say that Hitler was wrong to murder the Jews based on a personal opinion. By contrast, believers can authoritatively proclaim that murder is wrong based upon an objective third-party source outside of themselves that is applicable to all, not just themselves. For unbelievers to remain consistent they must say, "I believe murder to be wrong, but it may not be wrong to you. So I cannot tell you not to murder."

In summary of this illustration, developing epistemological discernment will enable you to wage your battles further upstream, where guns aren't loaded and opponents are the least fortified and equipped to defend themselves.

This is the dilemma of a subjective, self-informed epistemology versus an objective, God-informed Christian epistemology:

It's not your word against mine: it's your thinking against God's.

The believer is said to be God's *ambassador* (2 Corinthians 5:20). To the degree believers accurately represent the Book, they speak with the authority of God. Apologist Greg Bahnsen summarizes Van Til, a leading Reformed apologist, and his epistemological genius when he states, "[Unbelievers] face the challenge of justifying [their source of knowledge] with good reason."[3] Unbelievers use themselves as the source for determining what is right and wrong, and their opinions are thus devoid of any authority other than themselves. Nor are their standards enforceable on anyone outside of themselves. In fact, many an epistemology "is informed by an ethical hostility toward God."[4] When considering a bill in subcommittee or voting, take this into account: is this bill or candidate rooted in Scriptural truth, or is it based on subjective notions of right and wrong?

What is the underlying epistemology related to the presenting matter? That is the question! If you develop a smell for this, you will be wiser in the days and years ahead.

In subscribing to an epistemology based on outside revelation, I am always excited to get to the point in a discussion with a nonbeliever where I can ask the philosophical haymaker question: "So whom should I believe—your opinion or that of the Bible?" This is the essence of the epistemological authority question. It is always good to lovingly and kindly follow up with the comment, "Something to think about, isn't it?"

Believers do unbelievers a great service in helping them to clearly understand that their basis of authority is self and self only. It is this sobering exercise that can bring people toward repentance from pride and lead them toward faith in Christ. Paul has this thought in mind when he writes to the Corinthian believers in I Corinthians 2:14:

> *But a natural man does not accept the things of the Spirit of God, for they are foolishness to him.*

Why? Jesus states in John 3:19:

> *"Men loved the darkness rather than the Light, for their deeds were evil."*

Jesus goes on to say in the next verse that the reason unbelievers do not come to the *light* is that they do not want their sin to be exposed. Probing their epistemology can hopefully help some to begin to see their lack of any objective basis for what they believe. Romans 1:22 states in this regard:

Professing to be wise, they became fools.

Humility is a necessary, God-given first step in conversion to Christ, and effective apologetic argumentation can often serve to achieve those ends. Before some piece of legislation or candidate gets your vote, will they stand up to the challenge of justifying the source of their knowledge?

As for you, your knowledge is based on God's Word. Let's make sure we know its basic tenets so that we can stand on the solid rock of sound doctrine.

Notes

1 Copyright © 2016 by Houghton Mifflin Harcourt Publishing Company. Adapted and reproduced by permission from *The American Heritage Dictionary of the English Language, Fifth Edition*.

2 By permission. From Merriam-Webster.com © 2017 by Merriam-Webster, Inc. https://www.merriam-webster.com/dictionary/epistemology.

3 Greg L. Bahnsen, *Van Til's Apologetics* (Phillipsburg, New Jersey: P&R Publishing, 1998).

4 Ibid., 157.

Many people hold to some kind of religious "faith." However, the question we all must ask is, "Is my faith saving faith?" The Bible says that not all faith is saving faith (cf. Matthew 7:21–23). Therefore, the object of our faith is vital, and this is the reason I do not like the phrase that is often bantered about in politeness: "He or she is *a person of faith*." That is far too broad and doesn't really mean anything in terms of a person's eternal destiny. You can be a person of faith, yet not be saved! It is an indefinite term. The Bible says that our faith must be what is repeatedly referred to as *the faith*, with a definite article.

Understanding the Term: *The Faith*

If Scripture refers to true and saving faith in Jesus Christ as *the faith*, what then does God expect of His followers regarding the faith? This study will attempt to answer that question.

Notice in this regard Jude 3:

> *Beloved, while I was making every effort to write you about our common salvation, I felt the necessity to write to you appealing that you contend earnestly for the faith which was once for all handed down to the saints.*

Jude's epistle is best summarized as, "The Acts of the Apostates." Jude was Jesus' half-brother and converted after the resurrection of Christ (cf. John 7:1–9; Acts 1:14). In his single-chapter NT epistle Jude outlines the characteristics of false faith, which eventually defects, and calls all believers, even those in the Capital Community, to fight for the faith—*the* one and only true faith.

This important word combination *the faith* is pregnant with special meaning as it is used repeatedly throughout the NT. It refers to the whole body of revealed salvation truth contained in the Scriptures. It is used in Scripture with a definite article, not an indefinite one, in order to emphasize the singularity of true saving Biblical faith.

Scripture knows nothing of a religious philosophy that says, "All roads lead to heaven."

The last clause of Jude 3 reads, "*the faith which was once for all handed down to the saints*," emphasizing the finality of God's revelation regarding true saving faith—i.e., the Scriptures. "*Once for all*" the Scriptures reveal the way of true salvation, and are not to be added to or taken away from (Revelation 22:18, 19). That is to say, the faith is inalterable!

In contrast, cults always have three common alterations—an additional, supposedly authoritative "revelation," which in turn redefines two inalterable aspects of true saving faith: the person and the work of Jesus Christ.

The term *the faith* appears in the following NT passages:

Galatians 1:23

But only, they kept hearing, "He who once persecuted us is now preaching the faith which he once tried to destroy."

This is a reference to Paul, who resides in Arabia after his conversion, where he receives three years of instruction from the Lord. When he returns, the above passage is the response of the churches. Notice that they call belief in Christ *the faith*.

Ephesians 4:4–5

There is … one Lord, one faith, one baptism.

Here is an emphatic statement by Paul to the Ephesian church that there is only *one* legitimate saving *faith*.

Ephesians 4:11–13

And He gave some … as pastors and teachers, for the equipping of the saints for the work of service, to the building up of the body of Christ; until we all attain to the unity of the faith, and of the knowledge of the Son of God, to a mature man.

Notice the context of this use of *the faith*. It is associated with *unity*. Without doctrinal homogeneity, i.e., a common understanding of what the faith consists of, there cannot be unity in *the Body of Christ*. True Biblical unity stems from a common belief in the faith, which is based on sound doctrine. Further, notice from this passage that unity in the faith is transmitted through the under-shepherds God has given to His Church, i.e., *pastors and teachers*. As they teach God's Word, the followers of Christ are grounded in the faith, resulting in a unified Body of Believers. A failure to emphatically teach the singularity of genuine saving faith only leads to doctrinal confusion and division, and subsequent disunity of the Body.

Philippians 1:27

Only conduct yourselves in a manner worthy of the gospel of Christ, so that whether I come and see you or remain absent, I will hear of you that you are standing firm in one spirit, with one mind striving together for the faith of the gospel.

Here we see that *the faith* and *the Gospel* are synonymous terms, each with a singular definite article. Note what precedes these terms in the passage: "striving together" (*sunathleo*), which means "to labor." The word connotes a team struggling for victory against a common foe. This is the same emphasis Jude places on the faith in Jude 3. Again, note Jude's words:

I felt the necessity to write to you appealing that you contend earnestly for the faith which was once for all handed down to the saints.

One Greek word used in this passage is translated into two English words: "contend earnestly" (*epagonizomai*). It refers to an intense contest. The recurring application here is that the believer is to *labor* and *contest* with others who are misleading, in order to accurately preserve and convey the faith to believers and unbelievers alike. Jude, like Paul at the conclusion of 2 Timothy, is writing to refute the false teachers who are misleading many who need to know the way of true salvation. Accordingly, believers are to wage spiritual war against apostates, those who preach a counterfeit Gospel, which deceives and leads others astray. To cower from this task is to be less than spiritually mature in Christ and to play into the hands of Satan, who is the father of lies—i.e., the deceiver who leads many astray (cf. Revelation 20:1–3).

> It is therefore critical that ministries amongst Public Servants
> teach sound doctrine. Not only are individual spiritual
> destinies at stake, so are national policies.

First Timothy 4:1–2

But the Spirit explicitly says that in later times some will fall away from the faith, paying attention to deceitful spirits and doctrines of demons, by means of the hypocrisy of liars.

Paul's instruction to Timothy, who is pastoring the *recovering-from-false-teachers* church in Ephesus, presents a clear contrast between true saving faith—*the faith*—and false faith that cannot save, i.e., the *deceptive doctrines* of salvation propagated by lying, *hypocritical*, "spiritual" leaders. The *later times* refers to the period between the first and second coming of Christ (cf. Acts 2:16, 17; Hebrews 1:1, 2; 9:26; 1 Peter 1:20; 1 John 2:18). Therefore, this passage is descriptive of the prevalence of false faith in the age in which we now live, commonly known as the *church age*.

The Believer's Responsibility to the Faith

As we have already discussed in chapter 6, 1 John 2:12–13 is a wonderful passage for self-evaluation of spiritual maturity in regards to distinguishing true saving faith from false. As we have seen in Ephesians 4:4–5, Paul is defending the purity of the faith from that which is in error. That is precisely the same purpose in Jude's epistle, where he calls the Church to build yourself up "*on your most holy faith*" (v. 20). "Build" (*epoikodomeo*) literally means, "to build a house."

Peter adds perspective as he underscores this idea in his epistle to believers, charging them to always be "*ready to make a defense*" (1 Peter 3:15). "Defense" (*apologia*) can be translated as "answer." From this we get the English word "apologetics," which is "the branch of theology that is concerned with defending or proving the truth of Christian doctrines."[1] Together Jude and Peter charge believers to build themselves up with answers in order to maintain the message of the Gospel, being sure to be Biblically accurate for the salvation of souls! The sheer volume of these passages serves to underscore that ministries and ministers in the Capital must stand firmly on sound doctrine. How can you succeed as a believer if you do not prepare yourself with Scriptural truth? Could you compete in a congressional or senatorial election if you hadn't first prepared?

This was true in Old Testament times, when false worship brought a curse on Israel. It is equally important in our day that ministers and ministries on the Hill be characterized by sound doctrine. God hates false doctrine, and teachers who teach it can actually harm not only the spiritual lives of individuals, but the health of a nation. Sound doctrine is essential in order for God to bless our nation!

What role does the faith play in efficacious ministry on the Hill? I see at least three points:

1. THE PUBLIC SERVANT MUST KNOW SOUND DOCTRINE

Ephesians 4:14–15 says:

> *As a result, we are no longer to be children, tossed here and there by waves and carried about by every wind of doctrine, by the trickery of men, by craftiness in deceitful scheming; but speaking the truth in love, we are to grow up in all aspects into Him who is the head, even Christ.*

One commentator states well the intent of this passage: "Spiritually immature believers who are not grounded in the knowledge of Christ through God's Word are inclined to uncritically accept every sort of beguiling doctrinal error and fallacious interpretation of Scripture promulgated by deceitful, false teachers in the Church. They must learn discernment."[2]

That is a really powerful statement! First Thessalonians 5:21–22 echoes this warning to distinguish sound doctrine from false doctrine:

> *Examine everything carefully; hold fast to that which is good; abstain from every form of evil.*

Similar to the Public Servant's scrupulous analysis of every new bill presented in committee, the believer in the Capital must *examine* the veracity of *every* proffered philosophy. How? Colossians 3:16 states:

> *Let the word of Christ richly dwell within you, with all wisdom teaching and admonishing one another.*

Public Servants who are mature in Christ are characterized by motivated discipline in studying *the Word* of God. No longer are they dominated by a "what's in it for me?" idea of God's Word, or even "what devotional thought-nugget might it have for me today?" That is all fine and good, but one's quest for Scripture must go far beyond that. Christians seek the Word in order to sharpen and deepen their understanding of sound doctrine (cf. 2 Timothy 2:2). There must be more to our pursuit of Bible study than self-help; we pursue Bible study in order to gain and maintain sound doctrine.

2. THE PUBLIC SERVANT MUST BE ABLE TO DISCERN TRUTH FROM ERROR

First John 4:1 says:

> *Beloved, do not believe every spirit, but test the spirits to see whether they are from God, because many false prophets have gone out into the world.*

This attitude characterizes the Christians residing in Berea. Luke cites their craving for discernment regarding God's truth, saying:

> *They received the word with great eagerness, examining the Scriptures daily to see whether these things were so.* (Acts 17:11)

The word "test" (*dokimazo*) in 1 John 4:1 stems from the world of metallurgy, signifying the assaying of metals for the purity and value. Similarly, believers need to test all doctrinal teachings against the Word of God, possessing a critical eye of approval or rejection. Critical judgment, when based on a genuine spirit of love for people and not in self-righteousness, is not a negative characteristic. We assay most everything in life, from donut shops to marriage partners. What then is wrong with judging Bible teachers and their teachings? After all, spiritual teachings determine eternal destinies!

Matthew 24:5 and 11 add still more to our understanding of this matter. Jesus says:

> *"For many will come in My name, saying, 'I am the Christ,' and will mislead many."*

> *"Many false prophets will arise and will mislead many."*

Part of being *misled* or deceived is one's failure to realize it is happening, which stems from an underlying ignorance concerning the Word of God.

In Acts 20:29 Luke records Paul saying to the Ephesian elders before their encounter with false teachers:

> *"I know that after my departure savage wolves will come in among you, not sparing the flock."*

Even though Paul warns the Church leaders to *"be on the alert"* (Acts 20:31a), and even though he has spent three years building them up in the faith (Acts 20:31b), years later they are still deceived by false doctrine! It is subsequent to the takeover by the false teachers that Paul hands Timothy the keys to the Ephesian church: in 1 Timothy 1:20 we find that Paul throws them out! To possess the ability to discern spiritual truth from error is therefore a very important matter! Remember:

Since Satan is clever and beguiling, believers must be wise and discerning.

3. THE PUBLIC SERVANT MUST BE ABLE TO CONFRONT ERROR

Believers in the Capital must not only be grounded in sound doctrine and be able to discern truth from error, but they must be courageous in confronting false doctrine. Second Corinthians 10:5 states in this regard:

We are destroying speculations and every lofty thing raised up against the knowledge of God, and we are taking every thought captive to the obedience of Christ.

Here we see the active character that is Biblically appropriate in the war against false doctrine. In Hosea 4:6, God says of the spiritual leaders of Israel:

My people are destroyed for lack of knowledge. Because you have rejected knowledge, I also will reject you from being My priest.

This passage applies to believers today. God expects His followers to be loyal to Him! He does not look kindly upon believers who take an apathetic or passive view of defending the faith! Mature followers of Christ are not to be cowardly, sitting passively by in the locker room while Satan's false teachers run the field! In 1 Timothy 1:18 Paul says to Timothy:

This command I entrust to you, Timothy, my son, in accordance with the prophesies previously made concerning you, that by them you fight the good fight.

Paul is charging Timothy to remember he is called of God to be a *fighter* for the faith. Every believer should protect the purity of true saving faith, which is this: for each of us to put our trust in Christ alone for the forgiveness of sin.

In 1 Timothy 6:12 Paul echoes this theme: "*Fight the good fight of faith.*" The word "fight" (*agonizomai*) is the root from which we derive the English word *agonize*. It speaks of contending perseveringly against opposition and temptation, with the concentration, discipline, and extreme effort needed to win. In a larger sense, *the good fight of faith* refers to the spiritual conflict with darkness, a fight in which all mature believers are engaged.

Finally, Paul provides Timothy with capstone insights into successfully winning the battle for the faith. Second Timothy 1:13–14 states:

Retain the standard of sound words which you have heard from me, in the faith and love which are in Christ Jesus. Guard through the Holy Spirit who dwells in us, the treasure which has been entrusted to you.

These are two of my favorite verses. They sum up the most poignant aspects of leadership in God's work. "Guard" (*phulasso*) means "to protect." Paul refers to the faith as a *treasure entrusted* to Timothy. The word *entrusted* is comprised of two roots: *para*, "with," and *theke*, "to put." Combined they mean "to put with" or "deposit."

Paul calls the faith *the treasure*. God has *placed with* us that treasure and we are to guard it! Here is a beautiful picture of a tremendously serious responsibility. Properly understood this means that all believers, especially those who are leaders, have a sacred responsibility to be *protectors of the deposit*. That includes warding off those who would attempt to steal the treasure.

Knowing our Biblically mandated responsibilities, may we meditate on the gravity and sobering importance as believers of having been entrusted with the faith! We should crave sound doctrine and possess antennas for error. We must steadfastly guard and protect the purity of the faith. Remember it was our Lord who said of Himself, "*I am the way, and the truth, and the life; no one comes to the Father but through me.*" (John 14:6). Make no mistake here— every believer has been entrusted to protect and convey the singularity of true saving faith!

We cannot expect to see healthy Christians in the Capital Community if we do not first insist on Biblically accurate ministers and ministries!

Failing at this point means those who are charged with civil government leadership will be less than spiritually healthy and therefore less effective in leading our great nation. Let us not compromise, but insist on only the best in terms of Bible teachers and Bible teaching in our midst, if for no other reason than the health of the nation! Amen.

How you interpret the Bible shapes your worldview, which in turn impacts how you make decisions, live your life, and create public policy. Next we examine five very different methods of Biblical interpretation to help you better understand your own thinking as well as why other people think as they do.

Notes

1 Copyright © 2016 by Houghton Mifflin Harcourt Publishing Company. Adapted and reproduced by permission from *The American Heritage Dictionary of the English Language, Fifth Edition*.

2 John MacArthur, *The MacArthur Study Bible* (Nashville: W Publishing Group, 1997), 1779.

Be diligent to present yourself approved to God as a workman who does not need to be ashamed, accurately handling the word of truth.

2 TIMOTHY 2:15

CHAPTER 10

Can You Make the Bible Say Whatever You Want?

How many times have you heard someone respond to your Biblically based reason with, "Well that's a matter of your own interpretation." How do you respond when someone tries to neutralize your authoritative use of the Bible? How should you respond? Perhaps you've even given up using the Bible authoritatively because of this.

At the risk of sounding like a "smarty pants," I typically ask a question, lovingly, in response, "So, what school of Biblical interpretation do you subscribe to?" Understanding the five major schools of Biblical interpretation is important in order to gain wisdom and insight into how one's approach to Scripture affects personal beliefs and policy positions.

Hermeneutics is the study of Scriptural interpretation. In my years of ministry, I have discovered that most people do not realize there are differing schools of Biblical interpretation, let alone understand them. Let us look at these major hermeneutical schools to help gain a rudimentary understanding of each, because how we interpret Scripture shapes our worldview. For Public Servants, worldview is crucial! It informs the construct of policy formation.

Hermeneutics is the methods, techniques, rules, and principles that the student of the Bible incorporates in order to answer the question:

What does the Bible mean by what it says?

That is the vital question that hermeneutics attempts to answer. Like proper and improper exegesis of the United States Constitution, there must be a learned and practiced discipline in order to be effective and consistent in discovering what the author meant by what is said throughout Scripture.

You may remember that in the book of Proverbs Solomon often categorizes people into three general groups when it comes to wisdom (or a lack thereof): the *simpletons*, the *scoffers*, and the *wise*. As you study what follows, see how you would apply those monikers to those who subscribe to each of these hermeneutical schools.

The background of the word *hermeneutics* is quite interesting. Hermes was the Greek god who was said to have interpreted the message of the gods for mortals. Lest you think interpretation is a purely secular endeavor, the word is used by Christ Himself in Luke 24:27:

> *Then beginning with Moses and with all the prophets, He explained to them the things concerning Himself in all the Scriptures.*

In this passage, the English word "explained" is the Greek word *hermeneuo*, meaning "to interpret." It comes from the compound term *diermeneuo*.

Christ, the master of hermeneutics and greatest interpreter of the Old Testament Scripture, is talking to the two disciples on the Emmaus Road. As He interprets from the OT the things concerning Himself, their hearts became enlivened and illuminated as a result of the interpreter bringing the Scriptures alive to them (Luke 24:32):

There are approximately thirty-five Christian denominations that subscribe to this hermeneutic. The National Council of Churches and The World Council of Churches adhere to this interpretive approach.

HISTORY

Systems developed by Hobbs, Spinoza, F. C. Baur, and the Tubingen School of Criticism are responsible for birthing this hermeneutic relatively late in Church history. Those on the quest for the historical Jesus such as Albert Schweitzer and J. M. Robinson have also fostered this viewpoint. Many others in early America, such as H. E. Fosdick and other purveyors of the Social Gospel movement bear responsibility as well. Liberal hermeneutics grew in unison with the Social Gospel movement, also known as Theological Liberalism.

EVALUATION

- The Liberal approach is rationalistic.

- *Inspiration* and *supernatural* are both redefined. For example, since the human mind cannot explain miracles, the miracles of the Bible must therefore be discounted.

- The authority of human reasoning redefines, if not erases, much historically accepted Bible doctrine.

SUMMARY

With a Liberal hermeneutic, we arrogantly become the judge of Scripture, instead of Scripture being our judge.

The Neo-Orthodox School

OVERVIEW

Neo-Orthodoxy is an interpretive approach that denies propositional, objective, authoritative revelation. In justification of that premise, proponents of this school believe that the Bible is only infallible where revelation was given to the writers of the Bible—when God spoke it back then. And looking forward, Biblical inspiration only occurs subjectively "when God speaks to you through it now." Neo-Orthodoxy states that the Bible has instrumental authority because it is an instrument pointing to Christ, but it does not have inherent authority.

HISTORY

Names associated with Neo-Orthodoxy are Karl Barth (since its inception), Emil Brunner and Reinhold Niebuhr.

EVALUATION

- Neo-Orthodoxy denies the Bible is the Word of God and claims it *becomes* the Word of God only when God speaks through the Bible to a person and that person responds.

- Only that part of the Bible that witnesses to Christ is binding, and the authority for deciding this is the human mind.

- Many Bible episodes are treated mythologically, i.e., as teaching serious theological principles but not as having literally occurred.

SUMMARY

In essence, this school ends up destroying objective reliance on the Bible because it considers the Bible an unworthy, unreliable book. Both Theological Liberalism and Neo-Orthodoxy were founded upon archaeological and scientific evidences of several hundred years ago that brought Biblical veracity into question. Discoveries in scientific disciplines have since that time validated Biblical accuracy time and time again, rendering these two interpretive approaches outdated and myopic. The rug has been pulled out from under them. A rough parallel is illustrated from the discipline of geography: who would be deemed credible today for postulating religious beliefs based upon a flat-earth presupposition?

The Devotional School

OVERVIEW

This view regards the Bible as a rich book primarily given to nourish the spiritual life of the believer. Emphasis is placed on the edifying aspect of Scripture.

HISTORY

Many are those who reduce Scripture primarily to a daily "What's-in-it-for-me?" book of devotions. Among them are medieval mystics, Pietists, Puritans, Quakers, and familiar names such as Wesley, Matthew Henry, F. B. Meyer, and A. W. Tozer.

As one example, the Pietists movement was developed in reaction to the cold, stale, dead German Lutheranism of the late 1600s and early 1700s.

EVALUATION

- The Devotional approach focuses on application that is personally applied.

- There are dangers in zeroing in on narrow segments of the whole counsel of God; there must be a balance between the whole of Scripture and isolated application. Abuses include allegorizing, excessive typology, and neglect of prior doctrinal bases. One can isolate a single passage while disregarding context, thereby misinterpreting the authorial intent.

- Larger doctrinal constructs that give meaning to the sweeping themes of Scripture can be lost in the pursuit of the isolated snippet.

SUMMARY

Devotional hermeneutics does not honor Scripture as a whole piece, but narrows the focus in exchange for securing a quickly applicable thought that might further godliness in the life of the individual. It tends to underemphasize, if not denigrate, scholarship, for the gain of a quickly digestible, edifying idea. For the formation of good policy, the country is in dire need of Public Servants who have a deep grasp of the whole counsel of God.

Do you aspire to change the course of our nation?
If so, you need more than a devotional diet of the Word of God!

Another result of this minimalistic approach to understanding God's Word is that the door is often flung wide open to *eisegetical*[5] and *typological*[6] forms of interpretation. In contrast, the apostle Paul said in Acts 20:27: "*I did not shrink from declaring to you the whole purpose of God.*" Paul endeavored to get the big picture; so should we.

As in the case of the athlete who habitually consumes candy bars for quick energy while neglecting well-rounded meals, aspiring men and women of God must consume a balanced, high-protein Biblical diet, not just fast-food devotional snacks.

The Grammatical, Historical, Normative School (GHN)

OVERVIEW

In this last school, the meaning of a passage of Scripture is determined by what was thought to be the understanding of the words in the context of the time they were penned. The meaning is derived from grammatical and historical factors at the time of authorship.

It is important to note what this school is *not*. It is not characterized by letterism, or a wooden literalism.[7] Rather, it allows for an understanding of the author's use of varying styles, figures of speech, parables, metaphors, hyperbole, irony, euphemisms, paronomasia, proverbs, personification, oxymoron's, etc. In Latin this is referred to as *usus loquendi*, i.e., the semantics within a speech culture. In his classic textbook on hermeneutics Ramm calls this "the literal stratum of language."[8] The GHN school of hermeneutics recognizes *usus loquendi* and attempts interpretation with that in mind.

HISTORY

Ezra, the Jews of Palestine, and Christ all incorporate this discipline as evidenced from and within Scripture itself. Chrysostom, Luther, and Calvin subscribed to the GHN hermeneutic. Ezra in particular is the first OT example of such. The Jews have been exiled long enough in Babylonia to lose their native tongue; they are now speaking Aramaic. Ezra therefore assembles the Hebrew people and explains the real meaning of the OT text to them. Later in Church history it was the exegetical (lit. "to lead out") approach to interpretation that set the stage for the Reformation, as Calvin and Luther explicated what was actually in the Greek New Testament that had recently become available to the common people.

EVALUATION

- This is the usual secular practice in interpretation of literature. For example, Supreme Court justices who apply this approach to constitutional interpretation are known as *originalists*, while judges who read their views into the document are deemed *activists*.

- A large part of the Bible makes sense this way.

- This system exercises control over the imagination of the reader.

SUMMARY

Luther said, "That is the true method of interpretation which puts Scripture alongside of Scripture in a right and proper way."[9] Calvin said, "It is the first business of an interpreter to let his author say what he does say, instead of attributing to him what we think he ought to say."[10]

The GHN school of hermeneutics must be the thinking person's choice. It allows the Bible to remain untainted by subjective interpretive interference. This is the usual practice of interpreting past and present secular literature. It is the only school with a controlling force over eisegesis—our imagination foisted onto the Bible.

> The Allegorical, Liberal, and Neo-Orthodox schools of hermeneutics are the children of scoffers. The Devotional school is the brother of simpletons. It is the Grammatical, Historical, Normative school that is the father of the wise.

The next time a friend or fellow Public Servant quips, "That is a matter of your own interpretation," ask what hermeneutical school he or she subscribes to, and be prepared to debate the merits, or lack thereof.

Having identified a rational approach to Bible interpretation, you may be wondering how else rational reasoning plays into your Christian thinking. We'll explore that now.

Notes

1 A. Berkeley Mickelsen, *Interpreting the Bible* (Grand Rapids: Eerdmans, 1972), 28.

2 Ibid., 37.

3 James E. Rosscup, "Hermeneutics Syllabus" (unpublished, rev. April, 1999). Some of this chapter has stemmed from this godly man's work.

4 Ibid., 41.

5 *Eisegesis*: "the interpretation of a text (as of the Bible) by reading into it one's own ideas," By permission. From Merriam-Webster.com © 2017 by Merriam-Webster, Inc. https://www.merriam-webster.com/dictionary/eisegesis.

6 Bernard Ramm, *Protestant Biblical Interpretation* (Grand Rapids: Baker, 1970), 123–127. "[It] differs from a symbol or an allegory. It is a representation of an actual, historical reference. Often it relates to analogous fulfillment in Christ of OT stories and parallels. This was a very popular approach to interpretation in the Middle Ages."

7 Bernard Ramm, *Protestant Biblical Interpretation* (Grand Rapids: Baker, 1970), 123–127.

8 Bernard Ramm, *Protestant Biblical Interpretation*, 3rd ed. (Grand Rapids: Baker, 1975), 124.

9 Martin Luther, *Works of Martin Luther*, The Philadelphia Edition, Vol. III. (Philadelphia: Muhlenberg, 1943), 334.

10 John Calvin, *Commentaries on the Epistle of Paul the Apostle to the Romans*, translated and edited by the Rev. John Owen, Christian (Grand Rapids: Classics Ethereal Library), Preface, accessed March 15, 2018, www.ccel.org.

The fear of the LORD is the beginning of wisdom.

PSALM 111:10

CHAPTER 11

Rationalism, Rationality, and the Scriptures

All of us here on the Hill have chosen careers based on intellectual property. As a Public Servant your ability to execute vocationally is directly related to the agility you possess in reasoning. One observation I have made in ministry in the Capital is that this quality—the ability to quickly and effectively reason—separates the senior Members of the community from the novices. Solutions to social problems, ideas, the ability to persuade, debate, write, and speak, all depend on your reasoning acumen. Without it you're dust, as they say. With it you're a star.

Scripture is the foundation upon which all good reasoning is built. It is the only reliable foundation for all logic and good judgment. It is the only trustworthy basis for building ideas, actions, and practices. The Word of God is intended to be the mind's bedrock, its compass.

Rationalism And Rationality

As important as this is however, a distinction must immediately be made between two close English words: *rationalism* and *rationality*.

Rationalism is an anti-Biblical philosophy that is condescending toward Biblical Christianity. In contrast to the Biblically based rational thinker for whom Scriptural precepts inform the premise for what is ultimate truth, the rationalist sets up mind and ability to reason as both the source and final test of all truth. Mind becomes god, since personal mental faculties are authoritative over and above Scripture in the rationalist's way of thinking.

Accordingly, the rationalist denies divine revelation, whereas Christianity looks to the Bible as the beginning point of all reasoning. Scripture is preserved truth, untainted by *the fall* of man (see Genesis 3). At the fall, sin entered and affected the world to such an extent that it tainted human ability to reason without a bias toward sin. This is commonly referred to in theology as the *noetic* effect of sin.

> ### Unlike the human mind, Scripture is unaltered by the fall and untainted by sin.

Scripture has traveled the long road of time and is unaltered; the Bible is unstained by sin and its noetic effect on the mind of man.

The introduction of sin in Genesis 3 brought spiritual death not only to the soul of humanity, it damaged our intellectual purity as well. We possess fallen minds. This is evidenced by the fact that the closer we edge toward the arena of morality the more the noetic effect comes into play. The rationalist has not escaped the noetic effect of sin, but instead is either naïve or rebelliously rejecting of a Biblical premise.

In their pride, those who worship at the altar of their own brainpower consider themselves to be the starting point for the discovery of truth, and in so doing are categorically rejecting the Biblical truth that the mind is fallen. In essence they are attesting to what the famous French philosopher Jean Paul Sartre meant when he penned, "A finite mind without an infinite reference point is absurd" (although the atheist-Marxist probably didn't mean it the way I am interpreting it).

In summary, whereas Christians rightly reject the philosophical premise of rationalism, it must be made clear that they do not reject rationality. Rationality is the use of the mind, with God's Word as its foundation.

As Public Servants gradually master Scriptural truth, it becomes the ever-reliable basis for proper thinking—the foundation that enables them to make wise judgments and good policy, not only in vocational pursuits, but in personal life. That is precisely what wisdom and discernment are: sound logic, clear thought, and common sense based upon the mastery of Scriptural precepts. Scripture is the bulwark upon which all good reasoning is built. Everyone in the Capital needs to master the Scriptures in order to be truly wise in personal, familial and vocational life.

Vocationally, to proffer policy that has no Scriptural basis is to act foolishly and disserve the people of our most fabulous country. Reason apart from the Word of God inevitably leads to unsound ideas, whereas reason subjected to the Word of God is at the heart of wise policy formation. God wants us to use our minds based upon His Scripture; He wants us to be wise and discerning in all we do.

The Westminster Confession of Faith clarifies this when it states, "The whole counsel of God … is either expressly set down in Scripture, or by good and necessary consequence may be deduced from Scripture" (Chapter 1, Section 6). As you intently learn the Word, you will find that you are able to make sound and careful life decisions—and form policies—that flow from knowing and embracing Scriptural principles.

Interpret the text of Scripture accurately. Discover the context of the passage, the original authorial intent, and then apply its principles with sensible, careful, thoughtful, and Spirit-directed reasoning. These are the building blocks, the ingredients, of discernment. That's how you craft good policy.

That's *rationality*, not rationalism.

When Martin Luther was admonished to recant his teachings on the Bible regarding true salvation by faith alone (versus by the payment of indulgences, etc.), his response was illustrative of this very point. He said, "Unless I am convinced by Scripture and plain reason … my conscience is captive to the word of God. I cannot and I will not recant anything, for to go against conscience is neither right nor safe. God help me. Amen."[1] Luther's reasoning was based on the convictions he'd gained from studying Scripture.

It follows then that those Public Servants who spurn the truths, precepts, and great doctrines of Scripture are not wise or discerning, having not based their reason on sound footing. They may think they are wise, but they are misguided. In the end, their policies—home-crafted brews void of Scriptural grounding—will not serve them or the people well.

Now let us turn our attention to the Biblical passages that underscore this idea.

Selected OT Passages on the Need for Wisdom and Discernment

In the passages that follow, note the repetition and interconnectivity of the words *truth*, *knowledge*, *discernment*, *wisdom*, and *understanding*, and how they all stem from God and His Word.

Psalm 51:6

> *Behold, You desire truth in the innermost being, And in the hidden part You will make me know wisdom.*

This passage appears right after David acknowledges his sinful state, not only for himself, but for all of mankind, when he exclaims, "*Behold, I was brought forth in iniquity, And in sin my mother conceived me*" (Psalm 51:5). Even though we are innately sinful, God *desires* all to know His *truth* and then as a result, to live *skillfully*, insomuch as *wisdom* is the skill at living life for God's glory.

Psalm 111:10

> *The fear of the LORD is the beginning of wisdom; A good understanding have all those who do His commandments.*

The *fear of the Lord*, this passage states, is the *beginning* point of of skillful living—or legislating. A reverential awe and a submissive fear of the Lord are essential to wisdom. Without it we reject God's Word, concluding matters with our own minds (rationalism), devoid of any heavenly plumb line, standard, or premise. We become our own god.

Dr. "Well-I-think" becomes the source of knowledge
over and above the God of the Bible.

In order to be wise, we must exchange our own attitudes, will, feelings, deeds, and goals for those of the true God who has revealed Himself in Scripture; this is part of *fearing the Lord*.

Psalm 119:66

Teach me good discernment and knowledge, For I believe in Your commandments.

Note again the clear relationship between God's Word, *Your commandments*, and having *discernment* and *knowledge*. The premise of Scripture is that they are intrinsically intertwined. One cannot possess one without the other.

Proverbs 2:2–6

Make your ear attentive to wisdom, Incline your heart to understanding; For if you cry for discernment, Lift your voice for understanding; If you seek her as silver And search for her as for hidden treasures; Then you will discern the fear of the LORD And discover the knowledge of God. For the LORD gives wisdom; From His mouth come knowledge and understanding.

Accordingly, the *knowledge of God* is derived and achieved only from and by way of the study and application of His Book. Further underscoring the connection between the words of *His mouth* and the Bible is Paul's statement to Timothy in 2 Timothy 3:16–17:

All Scripture is inspired by God and profitable for teaching, for reproof, for correction, for training in righteousness; so that the man of God may be adequate, equipped for every good work.

The Greek word for "inspired" is *theopneustos*, meaning "God-breathed." The Scriptures are the actual evidence of God's breath.

Proverbs 4:7

"The beginning of wisdom is: Acquire wisdom; And with all your acquiring, get understanding."

I prefer the more vernacular NKJV translation of this passage: *"Wisdom is the principle thing; Therefore get wisdom. And in all your getting, get understanding."* This passage goes on to personify wisdom in verses 8 and 9 and list her benefits: *"Exalt her* [wisdom], *and she will promote you; She will bring you honor, when you embrace her. She will place on your head an ornament of grace; A crown of glory she will deliver to you"* (NKJV).

These are the tremendous benefits inuring to those who, as we read above in Proverbs 2:2–4, are *attentive, inclining, crying, lifting their voices, seeking, and searching* for God's *wisdom*. Why would anyone avoid such blessings? Start in on the habit of Bible study today and get blessed, my friend!

Now let us turn our attention to NT passages that underscore the necessity to reason from Scripture rather than building our reasoning on worldly foundations.

Selected NT Passages on the Need for Wisdom and Discernment

Colossians 1:9

> *For this reason also, since the day we heard of it, we have not ceased to pray for you and to ask that you may be filled with the knowledge of His will in all spiritual wisdom and understanding,*

Paul prayed that the Colossian believers would be "*filled with the knowledge of His will*," which is equated here with possessing *spiritual wisdom* and *understanding*. It is quite easy to discern God's will with your mind and your rational faculties when you have habitually and continually *filled* it with God's precepts from regular study. A *wise* person can therefore be further understood as someone who has accumulated and organized God's principles in order to automatically apply them in daily living.

Remember when you first learned to drive and how much concentration and effort it demanded? Now you drive almost subconsciously from regular practice and continual application of your state's driving laws. Wise living is parallel to this.

Whereas the world might call you an ideologue, Scripture calls you a person of conviction, someone who has a sure rudder! The principles of God's Word are inviolately infallible and indefatigable.

Colossians 2:3

> *In whom* [Christ] *are hidden all the treasures of wisdom and knowledge.*

This Pauline passage exclaims that "*all the treasures of wisdom*" are found in Christ. Our source for *wisdom* and *knowledge* is not found extra-Biblically in some other form. It is in Christ alone.

This is a bold statement given the context of Paul's writing: the Colossian church is being attacked by Gnostic heresy.

The Gnostics' viewed knowledge as something they singularly possessed. They saw their divine understanding as esoteric (knowledge that is restricted to a small group), as ancient day rationalists, if you will. Paul is refuting this erroneous idea that the Gnostics possess a secret source of wisdom and knowledge.

Like many rationalists today the Gnostics possessed an aura of elitism. They were the "haves," and others, in this case the believers in Colossae, were the "have-nots." Paul addresses their falsities by stating that *all* the wisdom of God and knowledge about Him are revealed through Christ and His written Word!

The Word of God—not human surveys, socio or physiological analyses, or other constructs void of Scriptural truth—should be your basis for policy formation and decision-making. Whereas history reveals that worldly epistemological bases are subject to the vicissitudes of time, the Word of God is unchanging.

Second Timothy 3:16

All Scripture is inspired by God and profitable for teaching, for reproof, for correction, for training in righteousness.

This passage, mentioned previously in relation to Proverbs 2, is deserving of stand-alone consideration. Literally, *inspired* means "God-breathed." In essence, another way to state this is, "all Scripture is given by inspiration." God divinely inspired or "breathed on" the writers of His Word. It is therefore a reliable foundation from which you can reason. It is your primary, superior basis for authoritative reasoning.

The wise Public Servant must regularly study the Word of God in order to have a lasting impact in service to the State. To craft policy that is not rooted in Scripture is to have a temporal rather than eternal impact, and is a disservice to the country. Reason from Scripture rather than relying on your mind alone!

Those who founded our great nation believed in the doctrine of the total depravity of humankind—that we possess a sinful nature from birth. They understood that government is necessary to restrict the sinful tendencies of our fallen condition. How important is this basic premise to the governance of our nation? That's what we will look at next.

Notes

1 John Piper, "The Final Authority: Are the Five Solas in the Bible? Part 6," October 3, 2017, *Desiring God*, accessed March 12, 2018, https://www.desiringgod.org/labs/the-final-authority.

These things I have written to you who believe in the name of the Son of God,
so that you may know that you have eternal life.

1 JOHN 5:13

CHAPTER 12

Rejecting the Doctrine of Sin

Scripture is clear that humanity is fallen. In fact, God ordained the Institution of Government primarily to restrain the sin nature of humanity; that is the primary reason government exists! To believe the opposite, that man is basically good, is to live in ignorance of Scriptural truth.

The late Francis Schaeffer, in his classic work, *How Should We Then Live?*, speaks regarding Michelangelo's famous statue of David located in Florence, Italy, that it is the artistic epitome of humanistic ideology that assumes that man is basically good. He quips, "If a woman were to wait to marry a living statue of David, she would never marry."[1] Michelangelo's statue, not to be confused with the real Biblical David, represents the humanist belief that mankind will ultimately ascend to perfection. But the humanists are wrong.

With ISIS massacring innocent and unarmed men, women, and children in the United States and other countries, we are naïve to think the world will become a better place by the use of reason. Not so. God ordained government to be a force to quell evil.

To improperly diagnose an ailment is to fail to cure it.

The necessity of any governing authorities' proper understanding of sin cannot be over-emphasized. Not only does the teaching of Scripture regarding this subject relate specifically to one's personal life, but it is foundational to one's professional understanding as a policy maker and law enforcer. Can you clearly think through the Biblical answers to the following questions?

- How do you explain the dual nature of humankind?

- Does sin infect and affect more than just the individual?

- Does sin infect and affect the whole world?

A Biblically accurate, informed understanding of sin will help you answer these questions. It is foundational to how you view the world and government's role, and is integral to the formation of a Christian worldview.

In this chapter we will focus on what the Bible teaches about the total depravity of mankind—the doctrine of sin. In that there are many passages on this subject throughout Scripture, I would like to zero in on those aspects that I think are most relevant not only to your personal life, but your thinking regarding public policy: how should a proper Biblical understanding of sin inform and influence your thinking?

First we will explore an accurate Biblical definition of sin, and then we will move on to its origin. Once we establish these fundamental premises, we will pivot to its manifestations, from individual sin to corporate, national sin.

Sin's Definition

When discussing what the Bible teaches about sin, and the fact that we live in a fallen world, an accurate understanding of what this means and does not mean is critically important.

I like conservative theologian Wayne Grudem's working definition of sin: "Sin is any failure to conform to the moral law of God in act, attitude or nature."[2] The Sermon on the Mount repeatedly makes it clear that sin is more than outward conformity to God's moral standards; it involves one's attitudes as well. For instance, in Matthew 5:22 anger is deemed sinful; in verse 28, so is lust. Additionally, while we *were by nature children of wrath*" (Ephesians 2:3), God imputes a new nature to the believer at the moment of salvation and expects us to live according to our new nature (cf. 2 Corinthians 5:17; 2 Peter 1:4).

Sin is more than self-centeredness. I remember one of my mountaineering friends in the tent next to mine in the middle of the night during a huge three-day windstorm at eighteen thousand feet elevation, asking me to help him memorize some Scripture. Half asleep, with chilled half-breaths, my first thought was, "How selfish of him!" Yes, he was being selfish, but he was expressing a *good* form of selfishness. In fact, much self-interest is approved in Scripture. When we are seeking to grow in our sanctification or to "*discipline* [our] *body and make it* [our] *slave*" (1 Corinthians 9:27), we are acting out of selfish desires. Yet God heartily approves of such things! Those are good selfish desires. By the same token, a person's *selfless* devotion to a false religion will not please God, much less attain God's standard of sinlessness. So selfishness is not a good one-word definition of sin.

Sin needs to be defined the way God defines it in His Word. Another way to understand sin is this: anything uncharacteristic of God that is present in us is sin. The Greek word for "sin" (*hamartia*) means "to miss the mark." Sin is to miss the mark of His perfect acts, attitudes, and nature. It is no wonder then that Paul states in Romans 3:23, "*All have sinned and fall short of the glory of God.*"

Sin's Origin

Sin was present in the angelic world before creation and the fall of man. This is evidenced by the fact that Satan and his demons rebelled and were cast out of heaven (cf. Isaiah 14:12ff.; Ezekiel 28:11–19; Luke 10:18) prior to the creation and fall of man in Genesis 1 and 3 respectively. Sin then entered the created world via the disobedience of Adam and Eve in the garden (Genesis 3:1–19). Eve trusted in herself and then Adam trusted in himself over and above trusting in what God had specifically commanded of them. They thought they knew better than God, in essence placing themselves above God and His ways (Genesis 3:5), and rebelliously promoting themselves to His place of sovereignty and authority.

Sin's Manifestation in the Individual

The Bible is clear that Adam's sin spread to each individual throughout all mankind. Again, Paul states in Romans 3:23 "*For all have sinned,*" the psalmist says, "*They have all turned aside, together they have become corrupt; There is no one who does good, not even one*" (Psalm 14:3), and Solomon adds, "*Indeed, there is not a righteous man on earth who continually does good and who never sins*" (Ecclesiastes 7:20). This is because sin is inherited from Adam. Paul explains it this way in Romans 5:12:

> *Therefore, just as through one man sin entered into the world, and death through sin, and so death spread to all men, because all sinned.*

Later Paul adds in v. 18, speaking of Adam and Jesus respectively:

> *So then as through one transgression there resulted condemnation to all men, even so through one act of righteousness there resulted justification of life to all men.*

In Romans 5:19 Paul adds this reference to Christ's work on Calvary:

> *For as through one man's disobedience the many were made sinners, even so through the obedience of the One the many will be made righteous.*

The best way to think about this is that in the garden Adam represented the whole human race that was to come. Unfair? God is God and this is the economy He chose.

> ### If we reason that Adam's imputation of sin is unfair, then we must also reason that Christ's imputation of righteousness is unfair.

Scripture teaches the imputation of both sin and righteousness: the former by birth as descendants of Adam, and the latter by faith. Notice the following passages: David best summarizes inherent individual sin in Psalm 51:5:

> *Behold, I was brought forth in iniquity, And in sin my mother conceived me.*

Paul teaches the imputation of righteousness through faith in Romans 3:21–22:

The righteousness of God has been manifested, ... even the righteousness of God through faith in Jesus Christ for all those who believe.

Furthermore, every part of the individual has been infected by and affected by sin. In that mankind possesses an inherent sinful nature, we have a predilection for, and commit sin. Created in the image of God—which explains any goodness we might have—we are nonetheless fallen, thus explaining our dual nature in a way no other philosophy can. The humanist's idealization of the statue of David as the perfect man expresses an impulse to seize on something that simply cannot be.

Throughout the ages since the fall, humans have carried the imprint of *imago dei*, or the image of God, alongside their inherited sin nature. The fall affected more than the souls of individual humans; in addition, it infected the whole world. Critically important is this: the governing authority of a nation must possess a working comprehension of the theology of not only individual sin, but of corporate sin as well.

Sin's Manifestation in the World

Equally important to the effect of sin on a personal level is its effect on the *whole world*. Many passages speak of sin's manifestation in the world, stating that the whole world is fallen, in contrast to defining sin strictly in terms of individuals. However, many conservative theologians stop at individual sin and do not develop the concept of corporate sin.

Conservative theologian Millard Erickson puts it best:

> The Bible teaches that evil has a status apart from and independent of any individual human will, a subsistence of its own.... We occasionally refer to this reality as 'the World' [*kosmos*]"[3]

Theologian Sasse adds that the Greek word *kosmos* is oftentimes used in Scripture in juxtaposition to the kingdom of God, i.e., *the world* is used by the Bible writers to depict the very embodiment of evil.[4]

THE FOUNDATIONAL PASSAGE

This expansive idea of not only individual but corporate consequences of the fall is seen in the immediate aftermath of the fall. Notice God's response to Adam and Eve in Genesis 3:17b–19a:

"Cursed is the ground because of you; In toil you will eat of it All the days of your life. Both thorns and thistles it shall grow for you; And you will eat the plants of the field; By the sweat of your face You will eat bread, Till you return to the ground."

The fall of Adam and Eve *cursed* not only them, but the whole earth as well. Have you ever wondered why nothing is easy in this life? It's hard to earn a living. It's hard to eat right. It's hard to stay in shape! It's hard to keep government on track! All serve to illustrate Genesis 3. Until Christ's return humanity exists in a fallen state, both in an individual and corporate sense. The second law of thermodynamics, entropy, came into existence with the fall: everything is constantly moving toward disorder, not perfection.

THE FUNCTIONAL PASSAGES

Jumping forward from Genesis 3 to the NT, the following passages teach this OT concept of universal fallenness, or corporate sin, through the use of the word *world*:

John 7:7

"The world cannot hate you, but it hates Me [Jesus] because I testify of it, that its deeds are evil."

John 15:18–19

"If the world hates you, you know that it has hated Me before it hated you. If you were of the world, the world would love its own; but because you are not of the world, but I chose you out of the world, because of this the world hates you."

John 17:14

"I have given them Your word; and the world has hated them, because they are not of the world, even as I am not of the world."

First Corinthians 1:21

For since in the wisdom of God the world through its wisdom did not come to know God, God was well-pleased through the foolishness of the message preached to save those who believe.

John 17:25

"O righteous Father, although the world has not known You, yet I have known You; and these have known that You sent Me."

John 1:10–11

He was in the world, and the world was made through Him, and the world did not know Him. He came to His own, and those who were His own did not receive Him.

Colossians 2:8

See to it that no one takes you captive through philosophy and empty deception, according to the tradition of men, according to the elementary principles of the world, rather than according to Christ.

John 8:23

And He was saying to them, "You are from below, I am from above; you are of this world, I am not of this world."

John 18:36

Jesus answered, "My kingdom is not of this world. If My kingdom were of this world, then My servants would be fighting so that I would not be handed over to the Jews; but as it is, My kingdom is not of this realm."

James 1:27

Pure and undefiled religion in the sight of our God and Father is this: to visit orphans and widows in their distress, and to keep oneself unstained by the world.

First John 2:15–17

Do not love the world nor the things in the world. If anyone loves the world, the love of the Father is not in him. For all that is in the world, the lust of the flesh and the lust of the eyes and the boastful pride of life, is not from the Father, but is from the world. The world is passing away, and also its lusts; but the one who does the will of God lives forever.

First John 5:4–5

For whatever is born of God overcomes the world; and this is the victory that has overcome the world—our faith. Who is the one who overcomes the world, but he who believes that Jesus is the Son of God?

Millard Erickson says this regarding the Biblical use of the word *world*: "The World represents an organized force, a power or order that is counterpoise to the Kingdom of God."[5]

It is clear from the use of the word *world* in all these passages that sin has infected and affected both individuals and the earth as a whole.

Applying this Understanding

TO THE INDIVIDUAL

First John 1:9 assures believers, "*If we confess our sins, He is faithful and righteous to forgive us our sins and to cleanse us from all unrighteousness.*" The believer needs to walk with a clear conscience, keeping his or her sin account current with Christ. That is to say, one cannot walk in the power and control of the Holy Spirit and at the same time continually quench the sanctifying work of the Holy Spirit. Whenever the Holy Spirit convicts your conscience you need to confess your wrongdoing to Him immediately in order to remain filled and empowered by the Holy Spirit. To do otherwise is to short-circuit His indwelling empowerment. Keep a short leash on your sin; keep erasing it from your life and thereby maximize your God-purposed potential in office and thereafter! It is normal for believers to be victorious over sin in their personal lives.

TO THE WORLD

The Biblical concept of corporate sin is an area especially important to political leaders and their formation of policy. Public Servants must view the world through the eyes of Scripture: that humanity is fallen and that government is meant by God to quell evil in the world, as we glean from Romans 13:1–8 and 1 Peter 2:13–14. Government is a manifestation of God's restraining grace in a fallen world. This hamartiological understanding (*hamartiology* is the study of sin) can radically shape a new understanding of your role in government.

To view the world as basically good and in need of *your* or *my* reasoning abilities, as if others will come to the conclusion to do what's right when convinced intellectually, is naïve, unwise, and at best viewing the world through rose-colored glasses. The unrest we have recently experienced around the globe only serves to illustrate the premise that if unchecked by strong governments intent on quelling evil, the fallen sin nature of man will increasingly run amok. Governments and their leaders must send a constant message that sin will be punished. When I hear of leaders trying to reason with terrorists who believe their deity commands them to kill us, I am reminded of Mark Twain's saying about trying to teach a pig to sing: it wastes your time and annoys the pig.

May this penetrate to the core of your understanding as a God-ordained leader in government. May your convictions be based upon a Scripturally solid understanding of sin. May humanistic naïveté come to an end in all branches of government.

Make no mistake: Humanity is totally depraved in nature. An America directed by the ideology of humanism will only become increasingly chaotic, whereas an America directed by leaders who understand the Biblical doctrine of sin will become increasingly peaceful. This is clear from Scripture and history.

There is a clear path to achieving the peace we seek in our nation, and that path is lit by the Word of God. The societal peace we seek begins within us as individuals, as we pursue godliness in all we do. Can God's Word help us to overcome personal struggles and sins, and to mature in our relationships? In Volume 2, Part III we will examine the pursuit of godliness in public service. We will see what spiritual growth and maturity look like, as well as facing head-on some of the temptations that "*so easily entangle us*" (Hebrews 12:1).

Notes

1 Francis A Schaeffer, *How Should We Then Live? The Rise and Decline of Western Thought and Culture* (Wheaton, IL: Crossway Books, 1976).

2 Wayne Grudem, *Systematic Theology: An Introduction to Biblical Doctrine* (Grand Rapids: Zondervan, 1994), 490.

3 Millard J. Erickson, *Christian Theology* (Grand Rapids: Baker Academic, 2013), 660.

4 *Theological Dictionary of the New Testament*, vol. 3, 1938 ed., s.v. "kosmos."

5 Millard J. Erickson, *Christian Theology* (Grand Rapids: Baker Academic, 2013).

ABOUT THE AUTHOR

Ralph is a third-generation Californian who grew up in La Mesa, a suburb of San Diego.

At 7'1" he played basketball for legendary Coach John Wooden at UCLA and was the first player to go to four NCAA Final-Four Tournaments. During both his junior and senior years he was an Academic All-American, graduating with a degree in ecosystems. He earned his Master of Divinity degree from The Master's Seminary some years later.

RALPH AND DANIELLE
DROLLINGER

After college, he turned down several NBA opportunities in order to play with Athletes in Action, touring the world and preaching the Gospel during the halftimes of their games. After four years with Athletes in Action he played briefly with the Dallas Mavericks as the first player they signed in the NBA expansion draft in 1980.

After his basketball days, he served in sports ministry as the director of the trade organization of America's sports ministry movement, Sports Outreach America. Ralph and his wife Danielle founded Capitol Ministries® in 1996 in the California State Capitol as a ministry to Members of the California Legislature. Capitol Ministries® has birthed dozens of ministries in capitols throughout the United States and the world.

In 2010 Ralph and Danielle launched Capitol Ministries® in Washington DC, where Ralph now teaches separate weekly Bible studies to Members of the White House Cabinet, Senate, and House.

Ralph and Danielle share three grown children, John, Susan, and Scott, and seven grandchildren.

Also by Ralph Drollinger: *Rebuilding America: The Biblical Blueprint*

Drollinger has authored hundreds of Bible studies that are specific to the professional, personal, and spiritual needs of political leaders. The studies are available free online at capmin.org.

And Jesus answered him, saying, It is written, That man shall not live by bread alone, but by every word that proceeds out of the mouth of God. (Matthew 4:4 and Luke 4:4 *The Four in One Gospel of Jesus*[1])

In 2016 Nordskog Publishing had the pleasure of publishing Ralph Drollinger's work, *Rebuilding America: The Biblical Blueprint*. That practical how-to book explores an important Biblical principle for restoring a nation, with insight and perspective from Scripture. I have been gratified to watch as Ralph and his wife Danielle's ministry has expanded as a vital presence in our nation's capitol, in most state capitols in America, and is now pursuing capitols in other nations of the world. These are times of great challenge for our country, with revelations of misconduct exploding onto the headlines and the ever-present war on Christianity steadily growing.

The timing of the publication of this book that you hold in your hands, *Oaks in Office: Biblical Essays for Political Leaders*, could not be more perfect. Indeed, here lies a remedy for all that ails our nation, and every nation. It is a systematic teaching of Christian doctrine, with an eye toward the unique concerns and challenges of public office. Public Servants seeking God's guidance through this book can rest assured that they are being tutored and shaped with the help of an author who stands securely and resolutely on the Word of God. There is no more firm foundation on which to stand than the truths that come forth from the mouth of God Himself.

My wife Gail and I, and son Daniel, visited Ralph and his wife Danielle Drollinger at their home to discuss this book program. Also present was Deborah Mendenhall, long-time friend of Danielle, and Capitol Ministries'® outstanding writer and editor. At that meeting I posed the question, why the title of the book, *Oaks In Office*? You can read his fascinating response, as he has eloquently laid it out in the Preface to this book. But I note that oaks also made an appearance in the Bible, and we can glean additional meaning from what God has to say about them in Isaiah 61:1–3:

> *The Spirit of the Lord GOD is upon me,*
> *Because the LORD has anointed me*
> *To bring good news to the afflicted;*

> *He has sent me to bind up the brokenhearted,*
> *To proclaim liberty to captives*
> *And freedom to prisoners;*
> *To proclaim the favorable year of the LORD*
> *And the day of vengeance of our God;*
> *To comfort all who mourn,*
> *To grant those who mourn in Zion,*
> *Giving them a garland instead of ashes,*
> *The oil of gladness instead of mourning,*
> *The mantle of praise instead of a spirit of fainting.*
> **So they will be called oaks of righteousness***,*
> *The planting of the LORD, that He may be glorified.* (emphasis added)

In Isaiah 61 we find a beautiful description of the Messiah that is to come, a vision of whom is granted to the ancient prophet some seven hundred years before the birth of Christ. Isaiah looks forward in time and sees a special individual who is to have the Lord's Spirit upon Him, and because of this anointing He will *"bring good news to the afflicted," "bind up the brokenhearted," "proclaim liberty to captives and freedom to prisoners,"* and *"comfort all who mourn."*

Rather than leave those who faint and mourn in the depths of their bondage, affliction, and brokenness, as in ashes, this loving Servant of God is to exchange their degradation for *"a garland," "the oil of gladness,"* and a *"mantle of praise."* Thus these poor souls are to become beneficiaries of God's favor. They will be called *"oaks of righteousness," "the planting of the LORD."* With nothing to bring to the equation, they are yet embraced and transformed by God such that they take on the attributes of the mighty oak tree, with its sturdy trunk, bountiful foliage, and steadfastness.

Seven hundred years after Isaiah wrote these words, when Jesus begins to minister in Galilee, he teaches in the synagogues, and indeed, the power of the Holy Spirit is upon Him. One day as He teaches in the synagogue of His hometown of Nazareth, it happens that the book of Isaiah is under discussion. He opens the book and reads this passage from Isaiah 61, and tells those assembled, *"Today this Scripture has been fulfilled in your hearing"* (Luke 4:21).

As you Public Servants pursue righteousness in your positions in office, may your eyes be opened as you study the truths of the Christian faith throughout this book, to see that Jesus Christ is indeed God's anointed, sent for the purpose of bringing good news, freeing prisoners, and binding what is broken. May your eyes also be opened to see that we are those wretches so deeply in need of His ministry. Without God's redemptive work we are afflicted, brokenhearted, and held captive by sin, but with His intervention we rise above our limitations to stand firm and stretch forth fruitful, joyful, eternal abundance of life, as *"oaks of righteousness, the planting of the LORD, that He may be glorified."*

This is no less true for those who are called to public service as office holders. You have something special to bring to your office, and it is bigger than yourself. Should you choose to represent God's vision for civic government, you will become a part of the fulfillment of His purposes and His will for the nation. We who follow God's Word crave to see America return to the godly principles of our founding. As Supreme Court Justice David Brewer well documented in the Supreme Court case 143 U.S. 457 (1892), our nation was founded based upon Christianity and the Holy Bible.[2] We have truly gone astray from those roots, but we are not without hope. If a generation rises up that is willing to earnestly seek the eternal truths of God and apply them in leadership, we may yet see revival and all the blessing that comes from obedience to God's will. *Will you not Yourself revive us again, that Your people may rejoice in You?* (Psalm 85:6)

> *The law of the LORD is perfect, restoring the soul; The testimony of the LORD is sure, making wise the simple.* (Psalm 19:7)

> *Your word is a lamp to my feet and a light to my path.* (Psalm 119:105)

> *For indeed we have had good news preached to us, just as they also; but the word they heard did not profit them, because it was not united by faith in those who heard.* (Hebrews 4:2)

> *Be diligent to present yourself approved to God as a workman who does not need to be ashamed, accurately handling the word of truth.* (2 Timothy 2:15)

Readers learning and applying these fifty-two in-depth Bible studies by Mr. Drollinger are Scripture-students in process of truly becoming Oaks in Office.

Jerry Nordskog

GERALD CHRISTIAN NORDSKOG
Easter Sunday 2018

Treasure these words of our Founders:

"It cannot be emphasized too strongly or too often that this great nation was founded, not by religionists, but by Christians; not on religions, but on the gospel of Jesus Christ. For this very reason peoples of other faiths have been afforded asylum, prosperity, and freedom of worship here."
— *The Trumpet Voice of Freedom: **Patrick Henry** of Virginia*, p. iii.

"From the day of the Declaration... they (the American people) were bound by the laws of God, which they all, and by the laws of The Gospel, which they nearly all, acknowledge as the rules of their conduct." — **John Quincy Adams** (Thorton, XXIX).

"[T]he Christian religion – its general principles – must ever be regarded among us as the foundation of civil society." — **Daniel Webster**, *Mr. Webster's Speech in Defence of the Christian Ministry and in Favor of the Religious Instruction of the Young. Delivered in the Supreme Court of the United States, February 10, 1844, in the Case of Stephen Girard's Will* (Washington: Gales and Seaton, 1844), 41.

"The Bible is the chief moral cause of all that is good and the best corrector of all that is evil in human society – the best book for regulating the temporal concerns of men." — **Noah Webster**, *The Holy Bible ... With Amendments of the Language* (New Haven: Durrie & Peck, 1833), v.

Notes

1 Nikola Dimitrov, *The Four in One Gospel of Jesus: Chronologically Integrated According to Matthew, Mark, Luke, and John* (Ventura, CA: Nordskog Publishing, Inc., 2017), 23.

2 Dr. Jerry Newcombe, *The Book that Made America: How the Bible Formed Our Nation* (Ventura, CA: Nordskog Publishing, Inc., 2009), 243–246.